The Witch's Book of Days

THE
WITCH'S
BOOK
OF DAYS

Jean Kozocari, Jessica North and Yvonne Owens

illustrated by Miles Lowry

BEACH HOLME
PUBLISHERS
Victoria, B.C.

This edition is published by Beach Holme Publishers, 4252 Commerce Circle, Victoria, B.C., V8Z 4M2, with the assistance of The Canada Council and the B.C. Ministry of Small Business, Tourism and Culture.

Cover Art and Illustrations: Miles Lowry
Cover Design: Paul Thomas
Production Editor: Antonia Banyard
     Sarah Dodd
Flourish on the chapter headings and the shield image on the back cover taken from *Vere Foster's Advanced Watercolour Drawing — ILLUMINATING*, Marcus Ward & Co., London & Belfast

Canadian Cataloguing in Publication Data

Owens, Yvonne
 The witch's book of days

 Includes bibliographical references.
 ISBN 0-88878-348-5

 1. Witchcraft. 2. Rites and ceremonies.
I. Kozocari, Jean. II. North, Jessica. III. Title.
BF1571.O94 1993 133.4'3 C93-091888-6

to the Trees

Contents

Foreword

The original standard of Time, in most societies the world over, was the fluctuations of the moon. Some of the oldest petroglyphs, artifacts and cave drawings that have survived are moon calendars, recording the phases of the moon as they revolve. The Babylonian cosmologists (the "Chaldeans") established the continual calendar of moon-phases, for general time-keeping, as well as for ceremonial purposes. This standard of time-measurement is based on thirteen lunar months of twenty-eight days each, plus one day, forming a synthesis with the solar, 365-day year. A similar tradition of lunar thinking underlies the "year and a day" tradition of Celtic societies, current legal language and convention, and Scottish, Welsh and Irish custom. Witchcraft also has traditionally used the "year and a day" standard for initiation.

The "month" (named for the moon), commencing on the New Moon, was divided into four seven-day quarters, or weeks. Each day was named for the planet that was most prominent in the sky as the morning star appeared on the horizon, and these names have come down to us in Latinized or Teutonic forms. Hence we have Moon day, Tiw's (Indo-Aryan Mars) day, Wotan day, Thor's day, Freya day, Saturn day, and Sun day. These conventions, obviously, were retained, but when the world-mind, or collective consciousness, shifted to emphasize solar (left-brain, masculine, outer, and manifest) values, the standard of time measurement was changed in many cultures. The thirteenth month was dropped, and the year divided into twelve periods of twenty-eight to thirty-one days, the seasons measured by the four solar events, the summer and winter solstices and spring and autumn equinoxes. The winter solstice became the important festival in this system, marking the return of the sun's presence in the skies of the northern hemisphere, growing to eminence at the summer solstice and was true of the Roman system, which was encultured into the Christian world-view in the Julian Calendar. This was later modified producing the Gregorian Calendar, which we still use for general purposes.

In fact, the lunar cycle is slightly over twenty-nine (29.53) days in duration, so the seasonal year is really somewhere between twelve and thirteen months long. There is no absolutely accurate format of time; solar, lunar, or sidereal (stellar) time cycles are all slightly elliptical. But there will be thirteen moons of a certain degree of fullness, whether it be new, full or waning, in each seasonal year, and this observable fact was important to agricultural peoples, who traced their fertility and growing cycles according to the tidal, magnetic and watery influences of the moon.

Celtic peoples, while aware of the solstices and equinoxes, gave emphasis to the "fire holidays," or mid points between these events, which gave form to the "Wheel of The Year's" eight Sabbats (sacred days). The fire holidays— Samhain, Imbolc, Beltain, and Lammas (or Lughnasad)—marked specific stages of the agricultural year, from seed to harvest. The premier festival of the "Old Religion," was Samhain, now known as Halloween. This gave the last harvest, the gleaning and winnowing, and the conservation of seed grain for the duration of the winter. Esther Harding points out in *Women's Mysteries* that the antique Briton's primary winter celebration was Samhain, and that it marked the beginning of the new year, with a focus on the storage and incubation of seed. There are folk-names for the thirteen lunations of the year that survive to us from British tradition, as shown in diagram.

The earliest Celtic pattern divided the year into thirteen months that were named for thirteen trees, as well as for thirteen of the phonetic sounds (consonants) that formulated the Ogham script, or that used by the Druids. The first month was Beith, or Birch, and commenced in the first final-quarter moon after the fall equinox. This was the original method by which timing for the festival of Samhain, or "All Hallows" was calculated. The ancient Celts' New Year commenced with this festival, and the timing of the event slid around with the moon fluctuations from year to year. A later Druidic tradition of the British Isles changed this so that Birch commenced the same day every year, where we observe the first of November, and the months were made longer. This conformed their system to the Roman, twelve-month calendar already in place in many parts of Roman Europe and North Africa, but left a short, three day "month" as the thirteenth month, Elder, before the cycle resumed on the first of November. (Modern witches still observe Samhain as "New Year's Eve," on the thirty-first of October.)

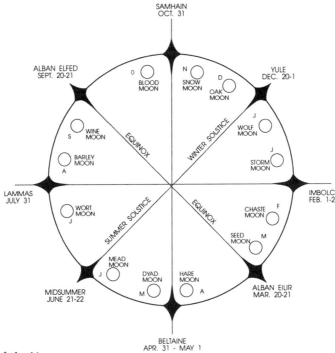

Wheel of the Year

The Controversy

A controversy exists concerning the placement of Birch month within the solar, Gregorian calendar. There are some who think that Birch (first month) commences with the solar New Year, in January. I believe that this tendency to place Birch month in January is based upon the seminal work of Robert Graves, *The White Goddess*, in which Graves said that he was assuming the first month fell in January. There are many within the Craft who have consulted Graves for the edification of their practice though he, by his own account, was not a Witch, Druid, or Celtic scholar per se. Although his work on the White Goddess was invaluable to the sum of knowledge generally, it was not concerned with witchcraft or ritual specifically, nor did he approach it from that viewpoint. His interest in the Goddess, in whatever guise, was primarily for Her function as Muse, for he was first and foremost a poet. He did not, therefore, need to be unduly concerned with exact, Sabbat placements; his accuracy was more concerned with poetic and lyric correspondences than the timing of ritual magic.

Celtic historians and practicing witches, however, know that the archaic pattern was to regard Samhain, or "All Hallows' Eve," as New Year's Eve, putting Birch month where we now find November. Samhain was the principle winter's festival, just as Beltane (now "May Eve," and directly opposite Samhain on the year wheel) was the principle summer's festival. Beltane falls in Oak month of the old system, which coincides with the influence of Taurus, and was observed with the garlanding of sacred oxen by the Druids. Celtic scholars, Liz and Colin Murray confirm this as a feature of the original Celtic calendar in their system of divination, "The Celtic Tree Oracle," citing the Coligny Stone (an early Roman attempt at solar/lunar synthesis) as a reference, among other artifacts. Gertrude Jobes, author of the *Dictionary of Mythology, Folklore and Symbols,* cites Alder month as the first month of the later Celtic solar year, confirming this view, for the terrestrial, solar year begins where we now find January, with the sun's increase, after the Winter's Solstice. In the symbolic system of ancient Britain, Alder is inseparable from the idea of Bran, the Celtic Saturn/Cronos, who presides over January as Capricorn.

I believe it is also primarily Graves who has influenced some modern Witches to construe the sequence of months as "Birch, Rowan, Ash, etc...," putting Ash before Alder in the cycle. This tendency is based upon Graves' citation of *The Ogygia* (by O'Flaherty) which claims an "authentic" orally transmitted tree-alphabet. This it may well be, though altered by time and the pressures of an overweening, solar/patriarchal World View. Graves also (in *The White Goddess*) cites numerous instances of Bardic epic poems (such as "The Battle of the Trees," and the poem of Talliesin) which show the sequence to be as we have it in *The Witch's Book of Days.*

There is also the historic (Druidic) habit of referring to the Ogham alphabet as "Beith, Luis, Nion..." to further complicate matters. My research suggests that this is a sort of nickname, or abbreviation, for the alphabet—which also encompassed an entire system of symbolization, known only to an initiate of the Druidic mysteries, and used as a Bardic frame of lyric and epic reference. The language of hand gestures was of paramount importance to a secret and exclusive society, members of which could communicate in sign language without non-initiates even being aware that any such communication was transpiring. There can be no doubt that the sequence of letters/trees/months would be accurate and meaningfully placed upon the hand, so as to facilitate this mnemonic signing—and there is no controversy or disagreement concerning the fact that the hand alphabet, whereby each joint of each finger represented a letter/tree/month and its attendant host of mythic correspondences, follows the "Birch, Rowan, Alder, Willow, Ash, ..." sequence.

The additional letters on the hand are "Q" and "Z." They stand for "Quert" and "Ztraif," or Apple and Blackthorn, and they share the months of Hazel and Reed. There are also the five vowels represented on the hand: "Ailim" (Silver Fir); "Ohn" (Furze); "Ur" (Heather); "Eadha" (White Popular); and "Ioho" (Yew).

4

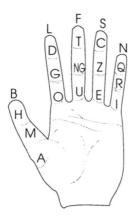

Lettered Hand

This still leaves us with the question, "Why was the hand language called the 'Beith, Luis, Nion?'" I believe that this is because the hailing sign among Druids and Witches was what Greeks and Italians call the "mullukya," and regarded as a protective sign. Druids and Witches knew this gesture as the "sign of the Horned God," and use it to hail each other in recognition. In this salutation, the hand is held in such a way that the only fingers extended or visible (thumb, forefinger, and little finger) are the ones that spell "Beith, Luis, and Nion," as pictured below. In this manner, reference to the alphabet included a reference to the religio-poetic order of initiates and their internal form of mutual acknowledgement at one and the same time. In all archaic, ritual/artistic systems of thought, multi-level puns of this type were tremendously important and signified bonds and deepened levels of understanding beyond the mundane. That later Druidic orders did become more solar-oriented and patriarchal is also apparent.

Sign of the Horned God

5

The Totems

The animals we have associated with the thirteen moons are amalgamated from several traditions. Some are taken from the petroglyphs left to us by prehistoric, thirteen-month calendar makers of the mound-builders of Ohio, Mississippi and Arkansas in the U.S. The speculations about the links between the mound builders, cavern painters and prehistoric artisans of these and other sites in the U.S. with early Phoenecian, Cretan (Mediterranean), and Celtic mariners are many—founded on the discovery of what resembles Ogham (Druidic-Celtic), Phoenecian and Cuniform script in these and other places ringing the Atlantic and Mediterranean. The sites of long-gone settlements in North Africa and Zambia have also yielded stone records of Arabic, Phoenecian and Ogham script.

Some of our animals are reclaimed from the earliest forms of the zodiac; for instance, the dragon (or horned sea-beast—from the ancient Babylonian image for the Capricorn Leviathan), and the tortoise (for earliest Cancer correspondences). Others are the creatures which matricist societies held most sacred and which more recent, patricist societies have reviled—the spider (Arachne—associated at one time with Virgo) and the snake (Urea, Ua-Zit, Al Uzza—associated by ancient Egyptians with Scorpio). The Bardic tradition has yielded some of our creatures, the Stag and the Unicorn (associated by Medieval poets and troubadours with purity and integrity) and the trees that corresponded with those virtues. Bees are associated with the Willow, due to the early appearance of catkins and the lure to bees they present. This fits well with the matricist vision of the bee goddess of old Europe associated with female industry and organization, fertility and established power.

These particular totems are by no means the only ones appropriate to the time-periods we have allocated them to, but they (or some version of them) can connect us to the thought-forms, and models for living, of earlier, less polarized systems and societies. They represent qualities and abilities within us, natural affinities and gifts, and aspects of Self.

The Hallows

The "Hallows" are the magical tools of the Craft of the Wise, or sacred Power Objects of Celtic Lore. The "Thirteen Hallows of Britain" were: a Sword (or spear); a Hamper of Food; a Drinking Horn; a Chariot; a Halter; a Knife; a Cauldron; a Whetstone; a Coat; a Crock; a Dish; a Chessboard; and a Cloak. Each related to a legendary motif in the sacred transformation system of the thirteen, tree-month stages of initiation into the British "Mysteries," and have their significance within the ancient Welsh myth cycle, called the Mabinogi, or

Mabinogion. The Spear is that which dealt the "dolorous blow" to Bran's foot (or thigh). The Dish is that which bore his severed head through the hall where he dwelt with his retinue for seven, mystical years—that it may keep them good company and prophesy. These motifs show up again in the Grail Myths, now converted to Christian mystical purposes. The spear, dripping blood, and the platter bearing a head precede the maiden bearing a miraculous Chalice in the Grail stories, the Chalice being a composite Cup and Cauldron and the primary symbol of the Mabinogi. The Cloak is the very same that lent invisibility to King Arthur when he made an heroic "underworld descent" (to Annwn, below the waters) in order to retrieve the Hallows, being principally concerned with the Cauldron of Regeneration. Despite their seeming variety, in their significance or function within the tales, the Thirteen Hallows reduce to four, primary sacred motifs: the Cup (or vessel); the Stave (or wand); the Sword (or blade); and the Disk (or pentacle). These, in turn, signify the four earthly elements of alchemical transformation: earth, air, fire and water. Witches turn to the four directions to invoke their characteristic, elemental energies, then to the center to address the archetypal, androgynous Self. This invocation can take the form of addressing the Lord and Lady, Goddess and God, the Universal Totality, or many other forms. These five points of focus are symbolized in the pentacle, the points being the four directions/elements, plus spirit, within the circumference of the World/ Self.

East is the direction of air, eliciting the qualities of mentality, analysis, definition, and clarity or exactitude. South evokes fire, with the characteristics of will and desire, intuition, energy, action and courage. West is the place of water, dreams, visions, all-inclusive Knowing or Gnosis, and all-encompassing experience. Feelings, mysticism and sexuality are also associated with the West, as well as the portal to the underworld, wisdom, and death. North is called the home of magic, for it is here that the energies of thought, intuitive will, desire, and emotion coalesce to manifest the changes, transformations or altered circumstances that the practitioner designs. North is the direction of the earth element, with the qualities of physicality, solidity, stability, and manifest form.

The magical, working tools that Witches use to engage these elemental energies are: the Athame (or witch's dagger or Blade) in the East to evoke the element of air and the qualities of Thought, mental definition and prowess; the Wand, or stave of wood, in the South to evoke the element of organic Fire and the qualities of Will, fortitude and desire; the Chalice in the West to evoke the element of Water and the qualities of Emotion, vision, and knowledge; and the Pentacle in the North to evoke elemental Earth and the qualities of solidity, crystalization, manifestation, form, and Magic.

The Druids called the four solar events, the summer and winter solstices and the spring and autumn equinoxes, "Albans." These occasions mark the year in terms of the hours of daylight available in the hemispheres of the globe. In the Northern hemisphere, the winter solstice is the shortest day and the longest night. The summer solstice, conversely, is the longest day and the shortest night. The spring and autumnal equinoxes are the points on the wheel of equal light and dark, with the day and night being equal. But they are pivotal points in that the light will grow from the spring equinox to its strongest point at the summer solstice, then decrease to the equipoise of the autumnal equinox, thereon to decrease daily up to the winter solstice. After the winter solstice, the light hours increase daily until they are again equal to the hours of night at the spring Equinox.

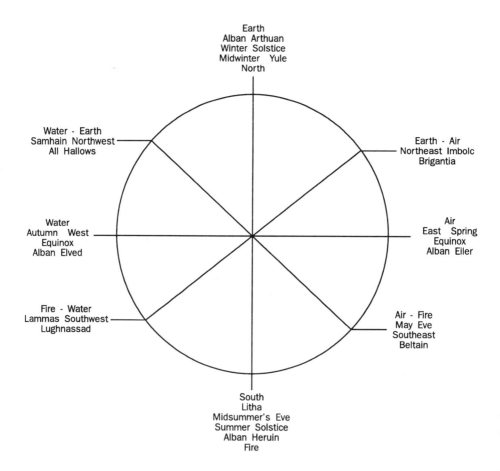

Wheel Image of the Year

In our wheel-image of the year, Birch is in the Northwest. The year of trees circles to the month of Rowan in the North, where the Winter Solstice occurs. The months proceed around the wheel to the festival of Brigid, in the first phase of Willow, then on to the Spring Equinox in the East. The next "fire-holiday," or Celtic festival is Beltane in the Southeast quadrant of the Wheel in second phase of Oak, and on around to the Summer Solstice in the South in the month of Holly. The next fire-holiday is Lammas in the Southwest in the third phase of the Vine month, then Autumn Equinox in the West during Reed. The eighth, and last, Sabbat of the year is Samhain in the Northwest in the last phase of Elder, followed by the single day, linking us again with Birch.

During the initial three months of the year, the months of Birch, Rowan, and Alder that span the Northern quadrant of the Wheel, let yourself become open to the finding of your pentacle or wand. The reason the direction of North/earth is also appropriate to the finding of your fire implement, the Wand, is because each direction/element includes its polarity, and one of the ways the cold, contracting, Saturnian nature of Winter/earth is propitiated is with fire. Depending on your own personal elemental make-up, including your astrology and chemistry, you may respond to North/earth/winter with fire, instead of by echoing it with earth. If this is the case, it should be allowed for, so feel for your inclination in this matter, and follow it.

In the three months that span the Spring Equinox (Willow, Ash, and Hawthorn) open up to the finding of your blade or your cup. As with the other polarity, air and water are propitiated with their like or their opposite, depending upon the affinities of the practitioner. Some may relate to Spring, as the quickener, or male blade—the impregnating "word." Others may identify with the vessel, matrix or womb, and resonate to the idea of the cup.

The blade can be anything from the standard Witch's black-handled, double-edged dagger to a ceremonial sword. This is up to you and your guiding forces. The cup, likewise, is a mystery until you find it. It may be a small vessel, a sea-shell, an ornate chalice, or an iron cauldron. All are appropriate, depending on you and the moment of recognition. In the Summer, cue yourself to find either the pentacle or the wand, whichever you didn't find in the Winter. Likewise in the Fall, find your cup or blade, depending on your choice in the Spring.

In the final month of Elder, the corridor, find your uniquely personal magical tool or tools. This might be a blank, black volume, in which to start (or continue) your Book of Shadows. This is the Witch's personal journal, where she traces and records her passage, complete with spells, rituals, visualizations, stories, graphs, correspondences, recipes, etc. The personal, magical tools of Alder could also take the form of the Crane Bag, the Druidic version of the mojo-bag, or shamaness's bag of tricks. As such, it could conceptually include all and any devices that serve, including language, symbology, tables of correspondences or significance, small stones, twigs, feathers, talismans, or jewelry.

We have allocated the single day, left-over at the end of the cycle, for the process of Self-Initiation. This is the moment when, collecting all of the sacred tools that have come to you through the year, including all the strengths, vulnerabilities, and realizations, you stand at the crossroads and make a decisive choice to walk the Path of the Wise. It is a profound decision, and not to be made lightly, for it means that life will never be quite the same as it was. Power is a joy and a burden, and comes with certain responsibilities. You will have had ample inklings of this by this time, if you have established a year's worth of connection and rapport with the moons and yourself.

The actual experience of initiation may occur at any time. It could be a carefully planned ceremony, or it may leap out at you from the depths of your unconscious in the form of a dream, or as a stream of synchronicities—a prolonged altered state. The more developed your lunar consciousness, the more clearly will these prime movements of the spirit present themselves.

In all shamanic, mystical traditions, of which The Craft is certainly one, there is the moment of Intitiation. This has been described as the mystical death, where the Self transforms and is reborn as one of The Wise. In this moment, we become the World Tree, or the Tree of Knowledge, the Asherah of our ancestress, the clan mother. The dynamic of this knowledge is within us, awaiting only our attention and resolve. May your journey be joyous, for your destination is assured.

Introduction

*T*he *Witch's Book of Days* is designed to serve as a year-and-a-day self-intitiation schedule. The organization of the year into four major segments between major holidays corresponds each of the segments to a characteristic element, direction, and magical tool, ie: NORTH—winter—earth—pentacle; EAST—spring—air—blade; SOUTH—summer—fire—wand; WEST— autumn—water—cup. The system of Days also revolves around solar events: the equinoxes and the solstices. The lunar calendar is a system of thirteen, twenty-eight day months plus a day, amounting to 365 days. This was the original system of time-keeping in most societies of the world. The Hebrew and Islamic sacred ceremonial calendars still employ a lunar system of time keeping.

The events on the following calendar pages were determined by a compilation of five books. In most cases, at least two books agree. Many dates were dependent upon moon phases, regional differences and energies released by the rituals. We have reserved the right to place some events on days determined by the traditions and the training of our Craft.

The practioner of lunar magic using this calendar starts at any point during the year, gaining and consecrating the appropriate tools, experiences and self-realizations in the appropriate time-frame. At the close of a year and a day, the initiate performs a self initiation ritual, the basis for which is provided (see Appendix A). *The Witch's Book of Days* is a guide to an orchestrated, terrestrially and celestially auspicious and empowered process of self-intitiation into the mysteries of the Craft, in the only manner in which it can be approached—by experience and with an investment of observation, introspection and time.

When you are ready to begin your journey of a year and a day, find the tree or lunar month that corresponds to the calendar month. Consult a newspaper or almanac to find the moon phases and mark them on your *Book of Days*. The full or "mother" moon represents the fullness or ripeness of the month. It is also the time when we are most emotional, intuitive and can even be considered by others as victims of lunar madness. On the contrary, to be kissed by the Lunar Goddess is a divine blessing, though it may be difficult to fully deal with at first. With practice, this "state" can become a time of great energy and power. Make a point to see the full moon each month and colour the moon as you see it. Sometimes it will be silver, sometimes goldenblood red, and at least once a year it will be blue.

The moon called the "first quarter" (just after the new moon) is considered the nymph or virgin moon, and is called "Diana's Bow." It is a time of beginnings for, like all women, the moon regains her virginity each month. When colouring the dark of this moon face, be aware that this is the solar or masculine portion of the available energy. The last quarter, or "Crone Moon," is a time to finish projects and to heal all wounds and make peace before rest.

The dark moon is named for Hecate. She is the Goddess of the crossroads and represents a time to choose a new direction. She deals with deeds that are best performed in the dark. The ending of unhealthy relationships and contracts may be easily achieved with Hecate's help. Originally, she was in charge of merciful death, abortion, and suicide. As you colour each day you will become aware of the change in solar and lunar energy and will learn to use it to your advantage. You can use your book of days to record your social life, but we suggest that you record your own thoughts and experience, especially in response to the daily texts. When you have completed the year and a day, finding your tools and celebrating each of the Witch's holidays (or "Sabbats"), turn to Appendix A to create a self-initiation ritual, having claimed your birthright as a Witch.

Blessed Be,

Jean Kozocari,
Jessica North,
Yvonne Owens

Creation Story

Jean—"In the beginning, there were no Goddesses or Gods. Places and objects had personalities and could be benevolent or malevolent, depending on a whim. When tribes or families formed working communities, two types of complimentary religions evolved. Solar or male religion concerned hunting for food and waging war for territory or slaves. Solar medicine or magic dealt with all nerve, tendon and skeletal injuries. Altered states of consciousness were achieved by gorging on food and fermented beverages after a hunt. Retelling and exaggerating stories of the hunt or battle was encouraged. Some of my female friends insist that nothing has changed. The same thing happens each week of football season. The men combined the greatest hero, the wisest man, most illustrious ancestor or favoured friend to represent the male energy or God. This image, however, was not powerful enough, so they took the strongest and most feared animal and combined the two images to represent the male God. In Africa, it was was the leopard, tiger, or elephant, but in Europe the great and majestic stag, combined with the male heroes, became the great Horned God.

"Women, busy during the day, found peace under the evening sky. The moon's cycle became a symbol—young, slim and virginal, then round, rich and full of blood like a pregnant woman. Soon it became frail and stooped like an old crone, only to disappear completely and return again to repeat the cycle. The women realized that the moon's cycle mirrored their menstrual cycle, and so the moon, or lunar energy, represented all women.

"Lunar magic or medicine concerned fertility, nutrition, and the digestive process. Herbs, food gathering, agriculture, hygiene, etiquette, and lunar time-keeping became the responsibility of women. The two religions complimented each other and continued separate but equal. The lunar season began at Beltane, when women provided fruit, grain, and young animals to feed the people. The solar or "male" season, when the men provided meat and game, began on Samhain—or "Hallow'een."

"Eventually the solar religion and its followers espoused a mathematical calendar with months of variable lengths, organized around the four solar events—the equinoxes and solstices. Women, for convenience, used the solar time system for their day-to-day life. Wise women, or "Witches," continued to live their magical lives by the lunar system of thirteen months, each ruled by and named after a different type of tree. You are cordially invited to turn the page and begin the journey to find the Witch inside you."

Birch

Birch is the slender, young sapling, the elegant new branch. It is intrinsically innocent, yet at the same time it is powerful and sophisticated with old-soul memory. It is pure in that it is entirely new, like a newborn child. But it is strong with innate knowing that comes through it from generations past, like the wisdom of ancestors. A very young child is often the most reliable source of true knowing—unbiased, as she or he will be, and unlimited by conditioned beliefs. This is the standpoint of Birch. The world, the wonder of it, its spiritual underpinnings, its manifest expression can be looked squarely and fearlessly in the eye. Old, no longer useful patterns can be thanked for their former value, and scrapped. Outworn relationships and structures that are not sound can be pared away.

The practice of "Birching," or ceremoniously flogging with a Birch switch, was used in Britain, and all across Europe and central Asia, to drive out regressive or decadent influences. This custom was followed in The Isle of Mann well into this century, applied to criminals. Initiatory practices of the Siberian shamans include "purification," or ritual scourging with Birch rods. The Altaic shamans, too, would be cleansed by leaping through a Birch hoop, and were required to demonstrate the ability to climb the World Tree in the form of a Birch pole.

This month is the time to adopt a "pure resolve," or intention to pursue The Path, or Way. This Way is the personal truth of the Seeker, or candidate for initiation into the Mysteries. If the resolve is sincere, the Way will open and your destination (Self-Knowledge) is assured. Integrity of intention is required, for nothing of value is attained without it. Birch speaks of all these capabilities. It is the tree of virtue and suppleness.

Jessica—"I spent some years living in the woods in the interior of B.C. Because I chose not to drive and because the roads were unsuitable for anything other than horseback riding, I walked a great deal. One of my favorite sights on the main road to anywhere were two extremely tall birch trees which stood side by side. I will always hold fond memories of the sight of these two stately trees, their golden yellow leaves shimmering in the autumn breezes in contrast to the many evergreen trees around them. In a land which is noted for its evergreen population, the birch stands out in her slender starkness during the winter months, her white branches reflecting the sun's rays and reminding us of the promise of spring when buds will appear and grow once again to maturity.

"Birch twigs have been used for making brooms. Birch has been used in saunas, beer has been brewed from her bark which has also been used to write upon in much the same way as papyrus. My treasure chest still includes some sheets of birch bark, still intact after many years."

A Hungarian folk-tale tells of a cow-herd who became worried when he heard the howling of wolves one night during a full moon. He went to the foreman, an old and experienced hand in such matters who was reputed to be something of a "Taltos," or magician. The foreman just sat smoking his pipe and appeared to be unconcerned. He told the cow-herd not to worry, that all would be well.

The cow-herd returned to the pasture, only to hear the howling coming closer and closer. He tried to heed the advice of the foreman but he found himself worrying just the same. Finally he went in search of the foreman, in a frenzy of concern about his herd. He found the foreman eating his supper, paying no heed to the approaching wolves. Then the foreman leaned back and lit up his pipe, showing no inclination to rise and follow the cow-herd out to the pasture.

Eventually, the wolves came right in among the cattle, circling around the choicest young steer. At last, the foreman bestirred himself to come out to the field. He carried with him his magical pouch and a Birch-wood hoop. As he approached the field, all the wolves sat down and looked at him expectantly. The foreman said to them, "Come on now, or it will be too late." And he made them all jump through the hoop as he passed a rag from the magical pouch over their backs, one by one. Then they ran off, looking back over their shoulders at the foreman, smiling with their long teeth. When the cow-herd asked the foreman what it all meant, the foreman replied that the wolves hadn't really wanted to kill a steer, they only wanted to get his attention.

"But why?" asked the cow-herd.

"Because if they hadn't jumped through my Birch hoop at the full moon,

18

they wouldn't have been able to turn back into men," the wily old foreman replied.

Asiatic shamans of Altai, Magyar, and Tatyar tribes (as well as others) employed a Birch hoop to transform or "shape-shift" into and out of animal bodies. This explains the incidence in Eastern European folk-tales of magical characters (or reconstituted shamans) causing wolves to pass through Birch hoops, that they have the ability to "turn back into men." The ability of Birch to "resurrect" the soul is reflected in these elements of folk and fairy tales.

The Rune for Birch is Berkano. "Berkano" means birch and also gestation, nourishment—the seed in the earth awaiting for the Spring.

The Gaelic name for Birch is Beith, and its letter is B. The symbol in the Ogham script is shown below.

Rune
Berkano

Ogham
Beith

Birch

1st Day	*All Hallows' Day, Birch enters trembling with fear, delight, joy, and anticipation. How and what are you feeling?*
2nd Day	*Emerging solar energy enhances assertive, orderly focus. Work with it.*
3rd Day	*Honor Hathor as Life Giver, the Womb. Lunar women go within to nourish the creation that lives within their womb, be it child, project, or relationship.*
4th Day	*Isis reanimates Osiris. Honor her by examining your solar and lunar desires and bringing them into balance.*
5th Day	*Light a candle to celebrate Wuwuchim Hopi fire ceremony for Nasaw the god of death and Spider Woman the mother of life. This is the balance you sought yesterday.*
6th Day	*Tiamat, your dragon mother, roars a message in your ears. What does she tell you?*
7th Day	*Lono blesses your first week's harvest and promises the reward of a new and fascinating friend. You.*
full moon	

The Birch Tree

The Priestess of Birch

Imagine that you are climbing a steep and rocky hill. It is a clear, dark night. The stars are shining brilliantly in the sky. Notice what phase the moon is in, as it rises over the hills. Ahead, in the darkness, you see a grove of Silver Birch. You can see their graceful, slender trunks gleaming in the moonlight. In the darkness around you, you sense the eyes of many small, wild animals watching. Within the grove of Birch trees that you are approaching, you know the Temple of Transformation awaits.

As you come closer, you begin to see the flickering lights of the torches and candles that fill the shrine. A gentle droning reaches your ears; the other Priestesses are waiting for you. You enter the trees, and see the Temple, bathed in torch-light. When you go inside, you see the Sybil, the Time-honoured Oracle of Delphi, seated within her precinct on her dais. Snakes are entwined around both her arms and they appear to be licking at her ears. She goes into trance as you approach and begins to speak.

"Daughter of the Oracle, your gifts of Sight, Smell, Sensation, Taste and Hearing will be enhanced. All that transpires you will Know and Understand. These and other gifts are yours; So Must It Be. You have the Tree of Ultimate Knowledge within you. It is yours, your birthright, and your own true nature. So Be It."

You accept the gifts of the Oracle and thank the Universe for your own design, which is sacred. Let your mind wander in its own pathways for a spell. When you return, come back to the everyday world by way of the Birch Temple of Transformation. Come back down the hill to your waking self, but know that you are transformed.

An active meditation for this month is to take into your hands a piece of plasticine. With your eyes closed, begin to shape it. Let your mind roam over the potential inherent in the raw shape of the year. The piece of plasticine in your hands is like the philosopher's stone, the potential of the Self.

Letting your thoughts and feeling control your hands, continue to mould and shape the plasticene until you reach a point of "completion." Then open your eyes and interpret what you have made. Subsequent studies of your sculpting may reveal other aspects of it, so keep it around for a while.

A passive meditation for Birch is to practice regarding everything and everyone around you with wide-open, non-judging eyes. Avoid categorizing people's actions or ongoing phenomena as "right or wrong," "good, bad, or ugly." Simply regard them as they happen, without any preconceptions. This will open up hidden aspects of surrounding events to your understanding, for the event will be catalogued and filed, before these more subtle aspects can be perceived.

21

This is a Self blessing, and consecration, to be spoken when the time is right:
"As above, so below
as the Universe, so the soul
as without, so within
Beautiful and Gracious, Goddess, One
on this day I consecrate to you
(Name)
Body, Mind, and Spirit
Blessed Be."

The mid-part of Birch month is home to the festival of Stenia, the "Bitching Festival." It is the perfect occasion for a contained fury, a choreographed rant, or an orgy of curses. These indulgences need harm no one. In fact, it is likely that steam released in this manner will reduce the potential of volatile emotions, resentments or irritations exploding in a hurtful or alienating way.

Jean—"During a summer storm, lightning may be dangerous but it is all the noisy thunder, while sounding frightful, that relieves tensions and really clears the air. Curses are the witches' equivalent of thunder. When exasperated beyond reason, a good euphonious curse is much more effective and satisfying than a stream of offensive profanity. Like the thunder, clear the air, release your tensions, and harm no-one.

"My Grandfather's favorite curse was seventy-seven in Russian. He claimed it was a perfect curse."

Birch

8th Day — *Ritual begins by moving deosil (clockwise or "sunwise"). As when winding a watch this creates energy and tension. Try to move deosil today. If your left hand is on the outside at each turn, you are moving correctly.*

9th Day — *Stir your beverage and brush your teeth deosil today, for these are also rituals. Record any changes in energy or emotions.*

10th Day — *What activities do you automatically do deosil? Are they satisfying and energy producing?*

11th Day — *The day to see the "Sidhe" (Pronounced "Shee"), or Fairy Folk, Lunantishees. If you don't see any today, write a story about them.*

12th Day — *Rosa Bonheor received legal permission to wear pants on this day in 1857. Do you need legal permission to be a witch?*

13th Day — *Stenia the Bitching Festival. Meet with a group of women you trust and take turns bitching to release negative emotions. Feast and wipe the slate clean. Karen Silkwood died, still accused of bitching.*

14th Day — *Feast of musicians. Play music that feeds your soul. What other hunger do you need to feed?*

The Priestess of Birch

The Hallows of Birch

The pentacle and wand are the Hallows of Birch, Rowan, and Alder. These are the implements of actively-willed manifestation. As such, they are more about pragmatic magic than the cup and blade of Spring and Autumn, which are more about inner alchemy. This is not to say that the wand and pentacle are not alchemical in their combination of earth and fire, or manifested Will. It is simply to say that the combination of the wand and pentacle might effect some more overtly material results.

An ideal magical working will, of course, include the energies of all four directions/elements/implements, for the clarity and precision of the air/intellect element, invoked by the blade, and the emotional fuel of the water/intuitive element, invoked by the cup, are also vital parts of every working.

Begin to tune yourself to the idea of your pentacle or wand. Are you feeling more the cooling, contracting, Saturnian earth element in this period, or are your feeling more the fire element with which earth and winter are warmed and illuminated? Take your time with this, for there are three months in which to sense your inclination in this matter.

Many symbols can serve as a pentacle for the altar. Sand-dollars have pentacles on their surfaces, a design in the shell. A dried, five-petalled flower is a pentacle. Any disk-shaped object has the pentacle shape inherently implied, and a rock, crystalization, or mineral specimen evokes the idea of earth's property of crystalizing primary ingredients into concrete form.

The traditional witch's pentacle is a disk with pentagram superimposed upon it. This can be crafted out of clay, fired ceramic, or metal. The metals associated with earth are iron and bronze. This is placed upon the altar (traditionally located on a North wall) in the direction of North, and is used to invoke the earth element and the Powers of the North. This actually means the powers of stability and form, the ability to manifest, that are inherent within us. "Invoking" is more a function of evoking energies in our own psyches. An altar can be any flat surface—a tabletop, or counter. It can be small and delicate, fooling visitors as to its actual role, or it can be grand and imposing, taking up half the room.

A wand might find you in this time-frame because of the inevitable dynamic of one element stimulating, and in fact, including its polarity. Wands come in all shapes and sizes. They are sometimes a delicate, sensitive, antennae-like branch or twig, and they are sometimes mighty staffs of Ash or Holly.

Yvonne—"I have an incredibly responsive wand of Hazel, which infallibly goes for essence and meaning in a thing, and is in fact made of the wood most often used for water-divining. Most prominent in my personal table of elemental influences, or my natal astrology, are fire and water, so all my tools seem to resonate to that. In other words, I have a fiery blade, a watery wand, a watery cup, and very mercurial pentacles of various types.

"You may find this kind of chemistry happening between you and your magical tools as well, so stay tuned-in to it and give it free rein. Jean points out that, depending upon your form of creative expression, a wand is often a pencil or a paintbrush. It could as easily be a mixing spoon, or a particular tree in the front yard. It is possible, perhaps even likely, that your wand will change, and be different things at different times. We've agreed that a wand can't be a typewriter or computer, however. It seems that a wand must be something that you can wield, in order to create, and a typewriter doesn't wield too well. This is not to say that a typewriter or computer isn't a magical tool, for it certainly is. A computer seems like an artifact of the mind or nervous system, and as such combines the elements.

"Another of my altar pieces is a 'Hecate Wheel,' also called the 'Hecate Pentacle.' It is made of red clay, is of a good, substantial size and weight, and evokes the stability and centeredness of the Earth element very well. Red clay is quartz silica suspended in water and has a highly organized molecular composition. It is like 'conscious' mud.

"I also use mineral crystalizations to evoke Earth. Their ultimate compression of matter which gives them the aligned, molecular density that renders them translucent and gives them their 'crystal' clarity also gives them a weight, or "gravity," that I find especially calming—even while it is enlivening, and seemingly stimulating to the nervous system. Also, the purity of color in gem stones resonate to the vibrational 'tones' (or frequencies) of the individual chakras. Quartz crystal is ideal in many ways because it is prismatic, having the ability to reflect the entire spectrum of visible light. Crystalizations are matter (materia, mater, matrix) at its densest and so express the earth element, which governs the physical plane, very well.

"Local native (Nootka) legend tells of the young initiate who was wandering in the forest to find his 'power stones.' He heard a clacking sound and, looking down, espied a number of crystals that were moving about, clicking against each other and making the strangely musical sound. He bent down and threw his coat over some of them and picked them up. He put them in his pouch and returned to his village, having found his power stones."

Birch

15th Day	*Georgia O'Keeffe, born 1887—her wand was her paintbrush, her chalice the arid desert. What wand did you use today?*
16th Day	*Hecate's Night. Re-explore the path you walked in the past year. Choose your new path. Where do you need to be?*
17th Day	*What anger did you meet on last year's path? Have you dealt with it?*
18th Day	*Release the Baba Yaga, the fierce witch power within you. Use your throat chakra. Scream or yell away your anger.*
19th Day	*Honor siblings and same-sex friends. Was part of your anger directed at them? Baba Yaga's power is truth. Was it your truth and would others recognize it?*
20th Day	*Indira Ghandi was killed by her body guards.*
21st Day	*Sun enters Sagittarius on or near this day. When you are honest and strong, who fears you? Are they close enough to harm you? Is the danger stimulating?*

The Hallows of Birch

The Totems of Birch

In early horoscopes, Snake was the Scorpio symbol. Our modern glyph for Scorpio (♏) derives from the ancient Egyptian hieroglyph for Snake: *Ƨɯ* . The period of the year ascribed to the influence of Scorpio roughly coincides with the ancient Celtic month of Birch. One of the attributes of Scorpio is the capacity for great depth, along with soaring vision. Scorpio can, in other words, dive deep into subconcious realms, or "the Underworld," then resurrect itself like a Phoenix, bringing realization, even revelation, from the depths. For this reason, the sign of Scorpio includes the Eagle, with Eagle's noble breadth of vision implied.

During the month of Birch, prepare to meet these capabilities within yourself. Like the slender, white birch tree, stand in the forest of events like a shining, newly rejeuvenated channel, with roots deep in old memory, and top branches high in the clear air.

Yvonne—"The story of the snake, the woman, and the tree is familiar to everyone. The tale has been with us for millennia, and in most of the early cultures where it was common, it had no negative connotation whatsoever. In fact, it was the chronicle of how we, as a species, came to be human. Free will is the issue, and it developed as an alternative to the automata of instinct, as a result of woman's attainment of objective knowledge, itself a result of the shift to menstruation from estrus (heats). No longer was sexual awareness consigned to a couple of weeks, every six months or so, as it is with other mammals of our size. Unlike any other creature on the planet (with the exception of some large primates), humans are sexually aware and responsive at any time in the cycle that they choose. Sexuality is, for us, a matter of choice, and this is as a result of the female of the species' shift to menstruous (men= moon, struous = course or way). This is the "Forbidden Knowledge" (Gnosis) that Judeo-Christian scripture damns as insubordination.

"Consciousness was so profoundly altered by this shift (later to be called "The Fall") when we as a species became knowingly sexual (ate of the Tree of Knowledge) and came to an understanding of Choice ("Good" and "Evil"), that it has to be regarded as an abrupt leap of evolution. Some of the resentment and ambivalence around the issue (shown in the condemming of the intitiative of Eve, for instance) is no doubt due to the fact that we are still reverberating from the shock, and its implications. We now have issues like ethics and free will to deal with, where once life was so simple and prescribed. We have creative options that other, instinct-ruled species do not. Our actions are dictated by our decisions, not our hormones (at least, some of the time). This turn of events was directly influenced by walking "upright," for it was then that the Kundalini conscious-energy rose in the spine to activate the entire nervous system with sexual energy from the base, or root, chakra, on a different axis, the "spine of consciousness." This phenomenon, this spiraling dynamic, is the Snake. It rises in the spine, connecting the Chakric system or energy centers (The Tree of Knowledge), with a coiling, serpentine motion, and endows us with the quality of consciousness we call "human." And so Eve (Lilith) is a heroine, not a villain—a triumph, not a liability.

"This dynamic of consciousness is the meaning behind the snakes that coil on the cadeuceus, or "Staff of Hermes," that medical science employs as its emblem, internationally, to this day. Hippocrates (and his Priestess predecessors in the Temples of Hygieia) were well aware of the Mercurial healing role of free-flowing Energy, and the physical health that is the result of the integration of the body consciousness. A major reason why trees are sacred to us is that they are a reminder of, and evoke, the core-connection of awareness inherent in us, from the roots to the crown of our inner being (The Tree of Knowledge)."

Birch

22nd Day

The law in Canada states, "You may not fraudulently pretend to practice witchcraft."

neu moon

23rd Day

We insist, "First pretend you are a witch, and you shall become one."

24th Day

"It's just your imagination; it's all in your mind." Does anyone say this to you to control or disempower you?

25th Day

Everything that exists was first created in someone's imagination. Thank the Goddess for your imagination.

26th Day

Use your imagination to light the fires of your life as a wish.

27th Day

Warning: You become what you fear the most. Do you fear your strength as Baba Yaga?

28th Day

Honor Hathor as Sekmet. Take a small orange, with your fingernail inscribe a crescent facing left, a circle, then a crescent facing right. This is the signature of the Goddess. Use it wisely.

The Totem of Birch

Rowan

The Rowan tree is the tree of psychic protection, and discrimination. Rowan branches were used for centuries to ward off misfortune, and still are in many parts of Great Britain. The Rowan is about integrity and personal sovereignty. This month can help you see and determine your own boundaries—where to draw the line, and where to conserve energy for your own nourishment. In former times, this quality of protection was thought of as the barrier to "enchantment," meaning undue influence or vampirism from outside oneself.

This is the month that leads up to the Winter's Solstice and so has the charge of inner experience. The borders of the Self are established so as to permit an inward focus upon the questions of energy conservation and personal choices. Rowan protects thresholds, and so the door between the inner and outer world is guarded, ensuring the peace of mind and tranquility to look within.

The observation of a commercial Christmas has befuddled some of the natural impulses connected with this month. This is the time when the natural world begins to pull back the outlay of energy in order to prioritize where and how it will be spent. Essential functions are the ones spotlighted, and choice and discrimination exercised to determine which functions these are.

Jessica—"Also known as European Mountain Ash and Quickbeam, Rowan is associated with witches, most notably in later days as a charm against bewitchment (but then, what is a more effective way to ensure the continuance of one's special tree than to claim its purpose is the opposite!) She was venerated by the Druids.

"Rowan wood has been used as a frame for bull-hide drums, for wands, for divination and as protection from lightning. Its berries, much loved by birds, contain vitamin C and have been used in the making of jams, jellies, pies and wine. Medicinally, the berries have been used in the treatment of diarrhea and hemorrhoids and as an astringent. (Please note: Medicinal uses of plants in this book are for historical interest only. Please consult a reputable herbalist for personal counsel.)

"My acquaintance with Rowan began when, as a child of 6, I lived in a residential and quite treed area of Montréal. I remember open fields, many Italian families with exquisite vegetable gardens and big Rowan trees with their stunning orange berries and elegant leaves swaying in the warm summer air."

The Winter Solstice, known to ancient Celts as "Alban Arthuan," will occur in or near the last moon phase of Rowan. This is the longest night and the shortest day of the solar cycle, but from this point the hours of daylight increase daily until the Summer Solstice when the process reverses itself. The re-emergence of the sun from its darkest hour was considered to be the rebirth of the sun from the womb of night. Alban Arthuan is so-called because Arthur was a Sun-God, and this was his birthday. Witches celebrate the Solstice as "Yule," from Scottish custom. The "Yule log" is burned upon this day, reminiscent of the rites of Mithras, when a flaming log of great size was ushered out of a cavern/womb as a symbol of the God's birth.

The sun also moves into the sign of Capricorn at the Solstice. The relationship of Merlin (Saturn/Cronos or Father Time) and Arthur indicate the Sun re-emerging under the tutelage of Saturn. Around the end of Rowan month Christmas occurs. The twenty-fifth of the solar month of December was the birthdate of Mithra, Saturn, Dionysus, Tammuz, Quetzalcoatl, Adonis, Attis, Frey, and Herne the Hunter long before the early Christian Church decided on this day for their psuedo-historical nativity of Christ. They chose this day precisely because it was the Mid-winter festival of the solar God in His many aspects and local forms. The sacred custom of millenia could not be eradicated so it had to be appropriated. Mithra, and his Vedic predecessor Mitra, was born on the twenty-fifth of December, in a sacred cave with animals, three Magii, and a heraldic star as a heavenly portent in attendance.

The Rune for Rowan is Laguz, signifying telepathy, wisdom, intention, communication with the collective unconscious, and travel on and communication with the astral plane, and Chiron (Sagittarius).

The Gaelic name for Rowan is Luis, the letter is L, and the Ogham symbol is shown below.

Rune
Laguz

Ogham
Luis

Rowan

November 29-December 5

1st Day *Honor Minerva, Goddess of craftspeople, teachers, artists and doctors. Wearing a helmet and carrying a shield and lance, she guards your path in Rowan.*

2nd Day *Mawu, African Great Mother and Hecate, Goddess of the Crossroad, help you to create order out of chaos.*

3rd Day *When Pallas, her lover, died, Athena placed her name before her own on all her temples so that Pallas would never be forgotten. Remember and say aloud the names of women you love and will never forget.*

4th Day *List the names of the women who taught you lessons in betrayal and treachery. Relive their actions and their lessons, then erase their names from your book and memory. Remember only that to betray another woman is to betray yourself.*

5th Day *Bona Dea, the Goddess of Justice for Women, banished all males from her rites—even cats. When you seek justice ask her aid.*

6th Day *With Chango, God of Thunder, Lightening and Drums, use your solar energy to drum up a storm.*

7th Day *Minerva blesses your talent. Begin to design a map of your perfect space.*

The Rowan Tree

The Priestess of Rowan

Choose a moon during the month of Rowan, either new or full, depending on your purpose; new for initiating a project, full for confirmation or completion. Prepare and take a cleansing bath. Create for yourself a sacred space, a Temple in an area where you feel safe and will not be disturbed. Burn some sage to sanctify and purify the area.

As you begin to envision your circle, welcome the Priestess within you. Feel her presence as you stretch out your arms and legs to form a human pentacle. Become aware of your personal space. This is the space occupied by you when you stretch your arms out around as far as you can reach without bending.

Feel yourself surrounded by a cone: envision it the colours of the rainbow— a large red base at your feet, then orange, yellow, green, aquamarine, indigo and violet. These are the colours of the chakras, the seven major energy centres in the human body—each representing particular functions or domains of earthly life, each with a different priority and way of performing in the manifest world. Notice the pentacle under your feet, the points extending to the parameters of your circle. You are the center where all things become possible.

What powers and abilities are incubating within you? Who or what feeds you physically? Who or what feeds you spiritually? What feeds your senses? How do you desire to feed friends, relatives? What celebrations, rituals or events further the clan or community bonds? How do you feed yourself?

These questions can be entertained this month, as you move through the days around the Solstice. Take the position of lovingly nourishing yourself. Discriminate, and choose only the best tea. Eat one piece of the best chocolate. Nourish and conserve your senses with beautiful music, fabrics, or settings.

What else feeds you? Sometimes what are construed as negative emotions feeds you. Anger and the sense of injustice can nourish right action. So-called "negative" emotions are simply emotions, and have a truth and veracity of their own. They are signs and indicators, and as such serve you by letting you know how you feel and where you stand. Honor all your feelings. Give them an absolute right to be.

This is not to say that one need suffer from rigorous feelings unduly, or be overcome by them. But you stand a far better chance of surviving your emotions if you don't deny them, for then they won't be relegated to the Shadow, to overwhelm you unexpectedly or sap your energy from behind a screen. Befriending the Shadow is another of the surest methods of psychic protection, for there will be fewer unacknowledged areas of Self that external programs can hook into.

At this point, look to see if you are burdened by the external programs of others. What are you carrying and why? If you feel ready to claim your freedom and release yourself from the expectations of others, imagine taking the hook(s) of their projections out of whatever part of your body they are attached to and letting them go back to wherever they came from. Allow them to go gently, with the words, "I willingly and freely release you."

It is more important and more appropriate to allow them to go rather than to track them to their source. Allow others the same freedom to release themselves from outmoded habits without interference or coersion.

Rowan month corresponds astrologically to Sagittarius, the Archer, who seeks to understand—whose vision is expansive and philosophic. Appreciate these capacities within yourself as you thank the Priestess who blesses you with the Goddess' understanding nature. Open the circle, with gratitude. Take these experiences with you as you move into your life.

Jessica—"I have always enjoyed the extremes of the Yule season. Perhaps it's the old Roman in me and memories of the Saturnalia; I see the over-indulgences of the season to be very life-affirming. Just when the Earth is closing down for a "long winter's nap," we humans are feasting and gifting one another and indulging ourselves in a way we are not likely to do at any other time of the year (and in a way that may take us a year to pay for!).

"What people who dislike the hustle and bustle may need to address is the looking within themselves which, to me, has also always been a part of this time of year. As we look within ourselves to discover anew and appreciate our own riches, it seems only natural to celebrate and to share our gifts, time, talents, and resources with one another in emulation of the earth's great bounty."

Rowan

December 6-12

8th Day	*You begin a new career by acting as if you know what you're doing. Today, act as if you were a witch.*
9th Day	*How did it feel? What did you do that was different?*

full moon

10th Day	*Immaculate conception of harvest deity means birth will occur in September, the second harvest.*
11th Day	*Celebrate Tonantzin, the Health Mother of Mexico. Eat only fruit and vegetables today. List menu.*
12th Day	*Inuit Feast to Sedna, Sea and Underworld Goddess, to appease the souls of killed seals. What will you serve?*
13th Day	*Bruma, the Goddess of Winter, flies on a broom leaving gifts for children and beating cruel parents with her broom. Give someone a gift.*
14th Day	*The Sun, worried because the people no longer played and frolicked, felt unloved and forgotten. He left the sky and travelled the world searching for someone who still cared for him.*

The Priestess of Rowan

The Hallows of Rowan

Rowan branches are used for metal divining, as Hazel is used to find water. Rowan is a frequent choice of wood for wands of every description, due to the intense, magical qualities, and what we would describe as Rowan's affinity for witches. The simple fact is that Rowan loves witches; there is a natural rapport between us.

Legends tell us that Faeries (or "witches") are inimical to iron, although the truth is probably more that iron, or The Iron Age specifically, was inimical to a magical/shamanic life led by early inhabitants of Western Europe. The Iron Age heralded their invasion by the chariot-riding Celts, or Indo-Europeans. Later, the Romans invaded with an even more structured and organized system of warfaring. The underlying reason why Rowan, the metal diviner, is the friend of witches is that it may have been credited with the detection of and protection from armoured invasion.

Rowan is one of the three, winter pentacle/wand months:

Jessica—"For a long time I would use any representation of the Earth element, from a potted plant to a bowl of salt, rocks, crystals, even herbs. Being a resident of the material, Earth plane, I am quite at ease with almost any material object being used for this purpose.

"It came to me one day a few years ago that it really was time to find a 'proper' pentacle. Of course, as soon as I made the decision to have one, there it was: a beautiful, hand-carved soapstone pentacle about 3" in diameter. According to tradition, I paid the price without haggling (which I don't usually do anyway. I am always ready to honor another's monetary value on an item. If I don't agree, I simply don't buy.) This pentacle now lives in a lovely silk bag on my altar, which it shares with a wide variety of crystals, among other items.

"I have always felt that we are living in a time of great expansion, especially in the area of consciousness. Therefore, while I have the utmost respect for limits and limitations, I also work to encourage myself and others to extend our reach beyond our comfortable little worlds. It was in this spirit that I decided to buy an unbounded, five-pointed star (a pentacle without the enclosing circle) to hang in my office window. It is made of stained glass—deep blue, the colour of intuition and of peace. For me it serves as a reminder that many things are possible. The Goddess provides."

To make a wand, first pick your tree. You may do this by deciding ahead of time what kind of tree you need, or simply by going out and looking around until one catches your eye. Then you must ask permission of the tree to harvest one of its limbs. Go into the auric field of the tree, close enough that you can feel its influence, then ask the tree if you may take a twig or branch to fulfill your purpose. You will know instantly if this is permitted or not. You will get a clear "yes" or "no" impression. If a particular tree is not agreeable, don't worry.

The right donor exists; it is just a matter of finding him or her.

When you've found your tree, take the branch or twig by moonlight, in the phase of the moon that seems fitting to your purpose for the wand, and to the integrity of the tree. Trust your own intuition in this matter. After you've harvested your branch or twig, thank the tree by leaving an offering at the roots. This offering can be anything that seems appropriate—a stone, feather, wine, water ...you will know. The wood can then be prepared in whatever manner seems magically and artistically right. You may want to trim and sand the wand until it is quite polished, or you may want to leave characteristic knots and bark in place. You might want to dress up the wand with beads and feathers, or with a crystal affixed to the tip. Or you may want to leave it in a more natural condition, perhaps with a veneer of oil or varnish alone.

When the wand is finished, consecrate it in a ritual. Light four candles, one for each direction. Make a pattern on your altar, a diamond shape, so that one candle is in the North, East, South, and West. Use a compass for this if you are not sure. Place the wand in the center, and whatever other talismans you feel will empower the Act. Call the powers and abilities of the four quarters into and out of yourself—clarity and vision in the East, initiative and will in the South, passion and intuition in the West, and power and stability in the North. Then draw from yourself the powers of feminine and masculine; address them as the Goddess and the God and make them welcome.

From this point of focus and power, take your wand up in your hand and bless it. Name it, and enumerate its powers and virtues. Dedicate it to the work you want it to perform for you, and charge it with this mission. When this process is complete, say, "The thing is Done. Blessed Be."

Then release the energies that you have called into play. First, thank and release the Goddess and the God. Although they are resident within you, they are not always equally, fully present. Say, "Great Gratitude. Hail and Farewell." Say something of this sort to each of the directions, working in opposite order to the way that you invoked the directions, i.e., first release the North, then the West, then the South, then the East. By the time you have completed this process you should have returned to "normal" awareness but, to be sure, always "ground" the energy after ritual. Go down to the floor or ground and place both hands, palms down, against the Earth. Allow the excess energy to flow from you, back into the Earth. Now have something to eat or drink. Nothing grounds and centers us like food.

Rowan

December 13-19

15th Day
Hawk Maiden begins her dance of rebirth dedicated to Spider Woman. Sit quietly in the dark. Are you Hawk Maiden or Spider Woman? Will you spin or dance?

16th Day
Halcyon, seven days before and after solstice should be calm and peaceful. Pay attention to your dreams which reveal hidden desires. Record your dreams.

17th Day
Honor Ops, Goddess of Plenty, by wrapping gifts in opulent paper. Seal each with her initial O made with a kiss.

18th Day
Doors sealed against the cold remained closed to the wandering Sun. One old couple took pity and gave him shelter, food, warm clothes and gifts. The sun returned to the sky, encouraged, and shone on the people once more. Sapienta—Goddess of Wisdom.

19th Day
Second night of Ops, for those who have forgotten to celebrate abundance.

20th Day
Begin to prepare for winter's solstice.

21st Day
Honor the Sun's demise, preparing for rebirth.

The Hallows of Rowan

The Totem of Rowan

Central Asian and Eastern European tribes, including the Tartars, Magyars, Mongols, and Turks, had a lifestyle that was perfectly efficient and that had cunning survival value for those who dwelt in the high desert valleys of the Russian Steppe, the plains of Hungary, and Transoxiana. This mode of life had been developed by early Aryan immigrants to the Iranian plateau (between Afghanistan and the Pamir Mountains) from the Upper Volga region and the Ural mountains. They developed this way of life in the several thousand years their tribes spent on the Iranian plateau.

This lifestyle was one that depended upon an absolute symbiosis with the horse. Marco Polo reported on his travels that the Tartar equestrians lived with their horses in the utmost severity of circumstances. On grave occasions they would sacrifice a horse, with great solemnity—as if it were a member of the family, and that then they would use every ounce of the horse's body in their fight for survival. They would eat the flesh, use the hide for tents, clothing and drums, the sinew for ropes and bindings, the hair, the hooves—everything. The main diet of the Tartars, Mongols, Magyars and other horse tribes consisted of mare's milk, cheese, and curdled whey. Fermented mare's milk and dried meat were their staples while travelling. When on a long trek across the unhospitable high desert, Tartar warriors would take their life directly from the horse's life; they would nick a vein in their horse's neck and drink from the stream of blood that flowed. Then they would stanch the wound and ride on. The horses apparently suffered this literal vampirism willingly for they were so devoted to their riders as to almost be a part of them. Those who have had a mystical relationship with a horse will understand the nature of this self-sacrificing bond.

It is to this tradition of symbiosis and sacrifice that we owe a rich tradition of fairy tale and lore from Russia and Eastern Europe that deals with the "Magical Horse." The chariot-riding Celts brought this tradition with them from their Indo-Aryan (Iranian) forebearers. The legends and deep felt religious beliefs in Epona, the ancestral horse totem of much of Celtic Europe, reflect it. The Mare Mother theme underlies the legends of Rhiannon, and Modron and Mabon are the sacred Mare/Mother and divine Colt/Son of the Gaelic Celts in Britain. The Mare Mother as tribal totem conferred sovereignty, and a horse sacrifice preceded Irish chieftains' assumption of rule.

Horses conferred status to Irish warrior kings as bulls conferred status to the matricist Irish queens who preceded them. It was over the matter of a brutal insult to the Irish king, the beheading of his royal horses by Evnissyen, that the original Anglo/Irish tensions were initiated according to Welsh myth. A white horse was an Indo-European symbol of the messianic return of the savior/hero, son of Mari (ocean), an idea that informed the psuedo-historical nativity of Christ. The final avatar of Vishnu is predicted to appear at the end of the world as a white horse, or riding upon one. "Horse-headed Demeter" touches upon this idea, as She is a later form of Rhea, the Mother Sea. The Black Mare is the "Nightmare," bringer of the foreknowledge of death in vision or dream. As the "Witch of the Westmoreland," she is the bringer of sexual healing. As the "Pooka," she is a fairy being who might drag the unsuspecting traveller into the watery realm of enchantment and death by drowning.

The month of Rowan coincides roughly with the astrological influence of Sagittarius, the Archer. This half-man, half-horse creature is Cheiron, the Centaur, from Greek myth. He is an archetype of the wounded healer and spiritual teacher, who brings divine understanding to humanity from the realm of the Gods. As such, he is a quality of motion and communication, governing the messages that travel among conscious areas of the body. Cheiron has been wounded by his own arrow symbol(consciousness) and the resultant wound is in the thigh (area of sexuality). He teaches Shamanic-magic abilities, like mastery over fire, and the ability to heal. The name of Rowan derives from Runa, a word that has the ancient Norse meaning of "magical charm," and the Sanskrit meaning of "magician."

A saying of the Shamans of the central-Asian horse-tribes was, "My horse is my drum." Both the horse and the drum were used to "ride" to other realms of the spirit, to bring back messages from the gods, or retrieve wisdom. The Shaman would sit, ear close to the surface of the drum, and enter trance while drumming. The rythm of drumbeats simulated the drumming of hooves and the sensation of travel, or flight. This flying-motion type of trance-state yielded visions, and the Shaman would return from it with teachings and messages for the tribe.

The horse is a vehicle and guide to divine revelations. With the sacred inner-space of self-defined and protected by self-determined, chosen thresholds and boundaries, allow yourself to travel this inner landscape. Don't be surprised if you experience the sensation of flight, your magical horse lifting into the air and soaring over myriad lands.

Rowan

December 20-26

22nd Day	*Hannukah—Tsao Chun, God of the Kitchen range makes cookies in the shape of stars. Let your solar part be a god and let your lunar part eat the cookies.*
23rd Day	*Winter's Solstice—Sun enters Capricorn—Awehai Kachina night dances. Dance with them for your footsteps are the heartbeat of mother earth.*
24th Day	*Chant: "Mithra, Osiris, Sunna, Amaterasu, Arinna, Kore, Befanna, Berchta!" It's their birthday and when you say their names they live again.*

new moon

25th Day	*Celebrate the birth of the undying Sun, in any way you so desire.*
26th Day	*Modresnach—Night of the Mothers. Like the Goddess who created the universe, your mother gave the world a marvelous gift. She gave us you!*
27th Day	*Christmas Day—Celebrate the rebirth of Buddah, Horus, Mitra and all male godforms born of woman—or those with belly buttons. The green yule tree, with silver stars, golden lights and crowned with mistletoe reflects the maypole in maturity and the rebirth of the undying Sun.*
28th Day	*Feast Day of Saturn/Lillitu. Eat of all good things that appeal to you.*

The Totem of Rowan

Alder

There is a feeling of nobility, strength, and great competence about Alder. The solar month of December ends and January begins during this period. Alder marked the commencement of the Celtic, solar year. The boundaries established in Rowan now protect the integrity of essential functions. The Northern Hemisphere is deep in Winter, and goes into minimal production, storing and conserving its vital force. Large animals enter winter sleep, and small animals hole up with their stores of nuts and grains. The fields are quiet, all activity taking place deep in the earth, unseen, in the incubation of seeds and the slow assimilation of minerals and nutrients.

We, also, desire to "hole-up," alone or with loved ones, go within, sleep, dream, read and think. This is the natural impulse of Alder. So is the impulse to prepare (and eat) feasts, celebrate bonds (or boundaries of relationships), and to do real magic. (While "bondings" are celebrated here, this was not regarded as a good time to initiate marriages, as it was considered part of the "dark" part of the year by ancient Celts.) The competence and form of the concrete, outer world is important now, so as to allow for undistracted musing, reverie, and revelry. There will be a desire for your house to be in order, simply so that you can escape from worrying about it.

The well-being of the Self, the clan, and the greater community has been furthered by the determining of borders, whether these borders be behavioral ground-rules, or simply remembering where the borders of one's personal territory lie, and where other people's concerns begin. It remains the most effective means of psychic protection to simply remember who you are.

Oracular power is associated with Alder. Here, the revelatory messages accessed in Rowan are spoken. There are the gifts of prophecy and clear sightedness. There is also the ability to protect oneself and one's clan in disputes regarding borders.

Jessica—"During one of my restorative sojourns in the country, I was fortunate to live among a great number of baby Alder trees. The land on which they grew was mountainous, rugged and the soil was very poor, yet the trees were hardy and determined. The nature of the Alder recalls to me my experience of my Scottish ancestors, members of the Douglas clan, and Alder herself has been used extensively in the building of foundational structures, especially those built under water.

"A great emotional homesickness for Scotland, a land which I have never in this life seen, surfaces every now and again, and I have come to recognize this as a visitation from my great, great grandparents—who emigrated to Canada and lived out their lives here. I feel myself to be a tribute to their determination.

"Alder is a water-loving tree whose wood is so oily as to be very water-resistant. Her wood was also used in the manufacture of wooden shoes and for water conduits. Medicinally, her bark leaves have been used as an astringent and to control inflammation and fever. A decoction of the inner bark, prepared in boiling vinegar, was applied to combat scabies and lice. Alder grows quickly so makes for effective natural fences, and she is also prized for she enriches the soil where she grows due to the presence of the nitrogen-producing bacteria which live at her roots."

The Alder Rune is Fehu, meaning moveable wealth, reputation, personal power, and possessions.

The Gaelic name for Alder is Fearn, the letter is F, and the Ogham symbol is shown below.

Rune
Fehu

Ogham
Fearn

Alder

December 27-January 2

1st Day	*First day of the Celtic solar year. Honor Freya, Goddess of Love and Fertility. Wear Brisingamen—a shiny sparkling necklace, and feed the cats who pulled her chariot.*
2nd Day	*End of Halcyon. Arachne spell: Choose a colored ribbon or yarn for each person close to you. Weave them into a braid to hang on your mirror. What will the spell do?*
3rd Day	*Chant to the nymphs: "Andromeda, Ariadne, Persephone, Kore, Abd, Ova!" Repeat throughout Alder month. Bubbulum is Woman's Day in Africa. African witches do everything backward. Try one simple thing in reverse. What did you learn?*
4th Day	*Beautiful and gracious Inanna is born this day.*
5th Day	*Solar new year fire festival for Pele and Mehuea. Light a candle at the water's edge.*
6th Day	*Three fates. If women pool their money to buy and light a candle to the fates tonight, one will find love, one success and one wealth. The fates decide which.*
7th Day	*In Japan, San Ga Nichi, three days without sweeping lest you sweep away good luck. Why are brooms so magical?*

The Alder Tree

The Priestess of Alder

Bran and Branwen were the ancestral heroic siblings of old Britain. They were to the Welsh like Isis and Osiris or Set and Nephthys were to the ancient Egyptians. Bran and Branwen are associated, along with their totem—the Raven— with oracular power. The power of their pronouncements can protect against invasion and conquest by outside influences, and preserve the integrity of the organism, whether that be the social organism or the personal self, body, mind or spirit.

During this period, practice spoken affirmations of your power to survive, and to thrive. State to yourself positive truths and perceptions. These may change daily, for nothing remains fixed, but you will readily begin to notice the power of pronouncements. So be careful what you things you say, for they will be manifest.

Choose the perceptions of inner truth that you wish to further, then state them as absolute truths to yourself. Accept these constructions without reserve, then let them go. You may even forget about them, until you notice that they are suddenly, profoundly manifest in your life, as facts.

For this exercise of oracular potency to work, the perceptions that you state must have been gained by sincere delving. They cannot be superficial perceptions, or frail "wishes." You must have genuinely gone within, and "seen" these possibilities within yourself, clearly.

After making an empowered statement of this kind, add the words, "If it harm none, So Be It." This gives you the added protection of being sure that you are harmonizing with the greater fabric of events, and ensuring that no shock waves be caused to rebound upon you and yours. The astrological set of Alder is Saturn/Lilith. The power to curse and bless is very strong, due to their contracting, solidifying influence. Energies want to cool, slow down, and manifest.

The Halcyon Days span the Winter's Solstice. They are calm, clear days when no storms blow and the surface of the ocean is flat and smooth. This serene interlude is named for Alcyon, who was transformed into a beautiful white kingfisher. Her name means "she who calms the storms."

Bran is the model for the Fisher King because he was wounded in the thigh by the "Dolorous Blow," and was lame thereafter. This resonates with the kingfisher's habit of standing in water with one leg raised as if lame. These characteristics informed the Fisher King of late Medieval legend, but their original model was the ancient king Bran, who dreams in the Western Isle. A counterpart of Bran is Cronos, another form of Saturn. The legend surrounding Cronos has it that he still sleeps in the misty Western Isle, and is even now dreaming into being this (physical) reality of ours.

Akkadian witch/priestess thought of Cronos/Saturn (Bran) as the earth-cave, from which the sun was reborn after the solstice. This accords with the myths surrounding Mitra, Mithras, Christ and others—as solar dieties born of a rock or rock cave. Merlin was the Welsh version of Bran/Cronos as Father Time and tutor/shelterer of the young sun, Arthur—as solar king.

Alder

8th Day	*How do you wish to be perceived one year from today?*
9th Day	*What tangible assets do you have one year from today?*
10th Day	*Draw a cobweb with thirteen spokes and connecting bands. Place your name in the center and the things you want to achieve at the outer edge.*
11th Day	*Spend time with a child, in memory of Babu, Patron of Midwives.*
12th Day	*Begin to collect and use seven magical herbs.*
13th Day	*With a piece of red yarn, tie a knot for each injustice to women you have observed recently. In the name of Themis, Goddess of Justice, sever a knot each time you protested inwardly or outwardly, ritually or conventionally.*
14th Day	*Two-aspected Janus guards your book of shadows, which are cast forward and back. You cast these shadows in the light of knowledge.*

The Priestess of Alder

The Hallows of Alder

A broom is a type of wand. It is a powerful tool in the clearing and sanctifying of magical working space. There is nothing quite like the feeling of having thoroughly discouraged regressive or impeding energies from lingering before the energetic onslaught of the broom. When you've cleansed a room with your broom, you know it.

Jean—"The first symbol of your acceptance as an apprentice comes when you are handed a broom and are required to sweep or clear a space to work, to learn, and to contain. Among Native American Indians, Haitians, Caribs, and Witches, new members of families or societal groups are required to sweep clean a working space. The first broom was a leafy branch tied to a belt or pulled behind a horse to wipe out one's tracks. This sweeping away of the past also wipes out old, outworn or undesirable loyalties or allegiances. The acceptance of the broom signifies your willingness to perform the tasks that will be your lessons and duties in the future. Unbelievably, there are homes today that hold no broom—the symbol and tool of witches and women.

"Set aside some time to purchase a new broom. A hardware, household or general store is the ideal place to start. Supermarkets and department stores are not conducive to to proper broom-shopping. Pass quietly by, with averted eyes, all brooms made of irridescent plastic threads or man-made fibres. Whisks of all shapes and sizes lead to real brooms made of real straw. My personal broom must have a green or yellow painted handle. The straw must be smooth and yellow, smelling like fresh-cut grass. Neat red stitches hold it firmly together. Try several brooms, do not choose until one moves trustingly into your hand and nestles there like a new lover. Choose carefully, for this is the beginning of an intimate relationship. Add to your purchase a small, child-size version, if possible. Pay the requested fee cheerfully, making no mention of how prices have risen. When you arrive back home, soak the broom in a pail (some homes don't have pails either) of warm water, to soften the straw and make it more flexible. Add a handful of salt to purify the broom in the name of the Goddess (Perhaps Hestia or Vesta—hearth Goddesses). Let it dry, with the head up, in the sunshine, and in fresh breezes. When you and the broom are ready, take it to your bedroom.

"Beginning in a corner, sweep. Feel the natural rhythm, like a dance... part waltz, part square-dance. Listen to the sound of it, soft, musical, and soothing— a rythmical counterpart to your own heartbeat. Carefully, craftily, collect feathers, cords, ribbons, beads, or feathers, and create a special gift for the broom—to be attached through the hole thoughtfully provided at the top of the handle. Later, on some moonlit night, take your broom to the lawn, woods, patio, or balcony. Hold the broom at arms length and begin to gavotte a pavane, turning in deosil (clockwise) circles, sweeping the earth briefly when facing the moon, and holding it aloft when not. When sanity returns, take your companion back to the kitchen and leave it face upwards, leaning against a wall, to keep the straw from bending. Be confident, she will keep your secret...

"When your broom is old, worn-out, and relieved of its duties, it may become your guardian witchlet or beldame. Sprinkle the broom with sea salt. Dip it in warm, soapy water, or spray it with your garden hose. When completely dry, attach a wooden coat hanger about four inches below the broom head, then begin to dress your creation in old but favorite clothes— the ones you can't throw out because you always had such a good time when you wore them. Petticoats, dresses, sweaters, blouses, skirts, belts, and scarves are all suitable. Jewelry or wigs are not appropriate.

"Bunches of aromatic herbs may be tucked into strategic spots to give a more lifelike appearance. Name it with a woman's name starting with BE or ME, and charge it with the work you wish to do. Place your manikin scarecrow or 'guyette' in a flower bed, garden or lawn. If you live in an apartment, place it on the balcony or behind the front door. There it will protect you from unwelcome guests, pests, or intruders."

Alder

15th Day	*Women made cream filled cakes in the shape of male genitalia and ate them in honor of Carmentalia, the Birth Goddess. Does sympathetic magic work?*
16th Day	*All Goddesses are one. We celebrate their aspects at different times in accordance with the energy of the season.*
17th Day	*Compiyalia—a time to honor your household. How do you?*
18th Day	*Druid feast of brewing. You need a small treat with a friend.*
19th Day	*Trifon Zarazan—Blessing of the Vine. Weave a circle of vine or string that has no beginning or end. Examine the circles in your craft.*
20th Day	*Consult your cobweb. Erase one band for each barrier to your goal you have removed. Any other changes needed? List them.*
21st Day	*Continue to consult your web, weaving and re-weaving as you create possibilities—or revise them.*

The Hallows of Alder

The Totems of Alder

When Bran The Blessed led his tribespeople in a bid to rescue his sister, Branwen, from a dishonorable marriage to the Irish king, he spanned an unfordable river with his gigantic body, forming a bridge for the army to cross over. The Alder tree grows in wetlands, and has an oily, water-resistant wood. It is used for ships, pilings, bridge supports, and foundation structures that stand in water or damp. The supports for The Tower of London, where Bran's Ravens were kept, are made of Alder wood.

These Ravens were associated with the perception that Bran's head, buried in the mound beneath the Tower of London, protected Britain against invasion or attack. When Bran's days of usefulness to his clan were at an end, he bade his followers to cut off his head (oracular power) and bury it where London now is, facing East, or the direction of the invaders from Normandy. This legend is the underlying reason for the presence of the ravens in The Tower of London, for the raven is Bran's power animal.

The Raven heralds portents. If there is something afoot, watch for the intercession of a raven, or adjutant crow, or blackbird. One of these birds chattering at you, dive-bombing or otherwise trying to gain your attention is a tip for you to hone your perception, and be alert. If you study the nature of the intercession on the part of one of these birds, you will probably have a feeling for what it is all about. They are signalling you about something your own subconscious perception, or oracular power, already knows.

Bran led the tribe to rescue Branwen because she had sent a Wren to tell him of her travail. Branwen trained a Wren to talk, so that she could send a message to her brother to the effect that she was not being honored in her marriage to the Irish King, but being daily humiliated instead. This little Wren was her totem and ally, and was one of the most sacred birds of the Druids because of this association. Wrens were studied for messages and warnings concerning the health and well-being of "the People."

The Kingfisher bird is a totem of Alder because of the association of kingfishers, the "Fisher King," "The Court of the Rich Fisherman," and the "Court of Love," or "Court of Joy" with the Court of Bran the Blessed. Bran, the Alder King, later shows up in myth as "King Bran" of the Grail Castle, where his cauldron of plenty is transformed into a jeweled, wondrous cup or chalice. The "Halcyon Days" occur near the first part of Alder, when the seas are so calm that Alcyon, in the form of a beautiful white Kingfisher, lays her eggs in a nest that floats upon the surface of the sea, while her mate stays lovingly by.

Another creature that is associated with this month is the mythical Dragon. Alder conforms roughly with the influence of Capricorn. In the Chaldean mountains of central Iraq once stood the city of Ur. In this urban temple-complex of the Summerian Goddess (Innana-Ishtar-Ashtoreth-Astarte) astrology was developed to an extremely refined degree—close to the form in which we recognize the art in the present day. The astrologer priestesses and priests were called, simply, the "Chaldeans," for this term conveyed all of their timeless tradition of mystical wisdom and science.

Their ancient system of astrology assigned the archetype of the horned sea-beast to the sign of Capricorn. This creature was more on the order of a water-dragon, or the Loch Ness monster, an archetype of vast, earthly power conveyed by the image of the Dragon or the Semitic Leviathan. Later (Greek) systems of symbolization reconstructed the horned sea-beast into the half-goat, half-fish of the modern zodiac.

The Dragon combines the earthly power of the elements and is like the land itself. It is mountain ranges, oceans, primeval reptilian memory, subterranean fire, raging winds, storms, and elemental force. It is a potent totem of Chinese medicine, magic and psychology, and is the divine, animal ancestor of the Welsh, the people of Bran The Blessed. Merlin is said to have been fathered by a Dragon.

The Dragon signifies ancient, genetic memory and survival acumen. Tradition and custom, tried and true methods and ancestry, are Dragon concerns. Dragons are also alert and wily and are reputed to hoard wealth in their treasure caves. Dragon can help you connect with the ability to be earthy, stable, materially secure and protected, structurally sound and in touch with your ancestral heritage.

There is a legend of the Nimpkish Band from Vancouver Island in British Columbia, about a fabulous sea-monster who lived in the waters of the Nimpkish River-mouth in the beginning of Time. Its name was Namxxelagiyu, and from its forehead grew a glowing quartz crystal. The legend has it that an ancestral hero encountered the sea-monster and struck the crystal with his harpoon. The force of the contact caused the hunter to swoon and when he recovered, the harpoon pulsed with a magic power. The harpoon was an indomitable weapon from that day forward.

Alder

January 17-23

22nd Day	*Seek Pax, Goddess of Peace, by making an apology. A witch admits her mistakes.*
23rd Day	*Sun enters Aquarius—solar religion changed Juno from queen, mother and patron of wives, to a jealous, neurotic shrew. Media continues the practice. Do you?*
24th Day	*Create a ritual to forgive the water for harm or floods. Janis Joplin and Dolly Parton share this birthday. What magic do they possess?*
25th Day	*Do a kindness for an older woman in honour of Baba Den, the Grandmother.*
26th Day	*List the nursery stories and songs that honored women and girls.*
27th Day	*Who are your heroes—male and female?*
28th Day	*Virginia Woolf Day—Alder is full of questions and change. Have you asked all the questions you need to ask?*

The Totems of Alder

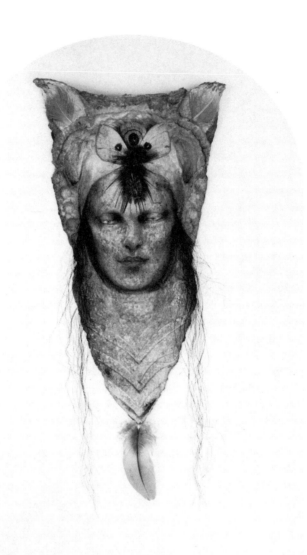

Willow

The willow tree is referred to in countless old folk songs and stories. In these stories, it is usually significant of a certain kind of female sadness—the grief of "fallen" women—having to do with maternity and abandonment, water and weeping. It was not always so. Long ago, in Britain and parts of Europe, in pre-Roman, pre-Christian times, there was no shame or sorrow connected with sex, menstruation, pregnancy, childbearing, or female independence. These were not reasons to be persecuted or ostracized, they were reasons to be honored. The Willow tree was a positive image of female fertility and power in this world-view. Lunar rhythms, the menstrual cycle, "night-vision" (intuitive giftedness), and female collectives were perceived in a favorable light. The Willow, significant of all these processes, was similarly seen as a joyful, sustaining image. By looking beyond the misogynist thrust of recent centuries, to the equitable Celts and earlier cultures, we regain this unburdened perception of Willow.

The festival of triform Brigid, pagan Ireland's Goddess of smithcraft, poetry and healing, occurs near the outset of this month. The original artifacts crafted out of metal were not weapons, but temple-wares, bowls, goblets, breast-plates, crowns, brooches, clasps, and other functional and ornamental devices. Metallurgy was considered one of the magical arts of the colleges of priestesses that flourished in Ireland, as well as many parts of Europe and the Middle East, along with poetic incantation, song, dance, and the ability to practice divination and healing. The magic of metallurgy was apparent in the careful crafting of crowns and breastplates. These were not originally merely insignias of rank, but functioned as psychic generators, with careful use of appropriate metals, and placement of gemstones creating energetic dynamics.

The female collective organization of the temple resembles the social organization of beehives: busy, intricate, organic, industrious, extremely fertile, nourishing, healing, and creating sweetness (honey/Art). The lunar/menstrual rhythms of large numbers of women in close proximity are said to have been the basis of the rituals and ceremonies of the Vestas, the priestess order of the Eternal Flame of Hestia, the Hearth Goddess, or Clan Mother. The moon cycle was harmonized with, in order to accentuate the particular properties and gifts of each phase of the moon.

One of the properties of the dark or new moon is called "night vision," the ability to see behind apparent reality and discern the energetic underpinnings. This is intuitive vision, a way to feelingly grasp causal factors. Occultists would call this "seeing beyond the veil," the veil being apparent reality, or what Vedic systems would call "illusion."

The Neolithic builders, who dwelt in this lunar, matrifocal world-view, built villages, towns, and burial-mounds with a collectivist logic, like beehives. This is true of the matricist societies of prehistoric Britain (earth-work mound-builders), and of peoples all around the Mediterranean, Old Europe, Anatolia (Turkey), the Middle East, the Arabian Peninsula, Persia, the Indian subcontinent, and across Transoxiana—or that swath of land that spanned ancient Kurdistan and Hindustan. The curvilinear lines of Sufi architecture still reflect this. The organic, connected interior space of the Minoans caused the solar-oriented, patricist warrior tribes of Northern Greece and Macedonia to regard it as labyrinthine and harboring of monsters (the Minotaur of Minos or "min," the Moon Bull). Tuned to outer manifestation and rational mind, left-brain functions, the invading warriors were threatened by the mysteriously coiling, organically-formed inner-space of the Minoan city and Temple complex, much as the right-brain, intuitive, subconscious or dream realm threatens those not habituated to it.

Willows are hardy and adaptable. They endure heat or cold well. The varieties of Willows grow anywhere from six to twenty-five metres, as in the case of the White Willow. Willow bark has been used medicinally for centuries, as an analgesic, disinfectant, and anti-inflammatory. Goddess-forms that are associated with Willow are Hecate, Persephone, and Hera. The planetary correlations are Venus and the moon. After Venus (sexual love) and the Moon (lunar, matrifocal beliefs like the lunar calendar) were damned as "demonic" by Judeo-Christian clergy, the Old English word for the various concepts: "willow," "witch," and "to bend," became the basis for a term for "evil,"—that being "wicked." The old word was "wicce," and also referred to baskets of bent willow, or wicker.

The Holy Day sacred to Brigid, Irish Goddess of smithcraft, poetry and healing, occurs during Willow. Their are many ways to celebrate the energetic and awakening qualities of this Sabbat.

Jessica—"One year I decided to invite a few friends to my home to celebrate Brigid Day with my family. I instructed everyone to bring candles color-co-ordinated to the wishes or plans they had for themselves that year. We had a wonderful potluck dinner, after which we all formed a circle, lit our candles as we spoke of our plans and filed out onto the front steps of the house in which I was living. Whenever the wind blew out our candles, we would allow another of the participants to re-light them while re-affirming our wish or desire."

The Willow Rune is Sowelo and signifies feminine perspective, feminine power, and the feminine aspect of the sun (or the reflected light of the sun upon the moon—moonlight).

The Gaelic name for Willow is Saille, the letter is S, and the Ogham symbol is shown below.

Rune
Sowelo

Ogham
Saille

Willow

1st Day	This is the start of the burgeoning time—last resistance of solar energy against unfolding female fertility.
2nd Day	While your Dionysus energy wants to indulge and amuse you, the Matronit/Ashtoreth/Lilith energy demands that you prune the trees and other growing things, including your lifestyle.
3rd Day	The god, Pan, causes sudden overwhelming fear or excitement, panic or joy. Do not panic over the abundance that is coming.
4th Day	During the Roman Sementivae Feria, count your seeds or talents. Plan to study an occult art—tarot, palmistry, or numerology.
5th Day	Paganalia—Prepare your mind as a gardener prepares the earth.
6th Day	Who are the witches? Where do they come from? Maybe your great-great grandmother was one. Research the crones in your family. Learn their stories.
7th Day	Celebrate with Bonfim, the Mexican Goddess of Happy Endings, even if you don't feel it. Discipline yourself to accept happiness.

The Willow Tree

The Priestess of Willow

In the month of Willow, prepare to find vast resources of historic and ancestral female power within yourself. Ancient memory may surface here, to connect you with your heritage, that of the civilization-builders. Every art and every science, from writing to agriculture to metallurgy to astronomy, was first developed while the Goddess was worshiped as premier deity. When the Roman church permitted the worship of Mary in the twelfth century (after having banned it since the sixth century), an invigoration of culture occured that was so profound that it is referred to by art historians as "The Flowering of The Middle Ages." The building of the great cathederals was begun in this period, all of them dedicated to Mary. The concept of chivalry and courtly love was born, and the convention of composing worshipful poetry to "the Gracious Lady." Many of her most ardent worshippers made little distinction between Mary and Isis, and were later regarded as heretical. This group includes the Cathari, Merovingians, and Gnostics, and they reconstituted precisely the kind of ardent, integrated, and highly cultivated Goddess-worship the church most feared.

Consciousness of the ancient tradition from which we are descended may become very clear. Allow yourself to remember the thriving, cultured, industrious, and comfort-oriented (even opulent) cities of the matrifocal Age of Taurus, the Moon Bull (5,000-3,000 BC approximately). These were cities built on the assumption of constructive, peaceful activity, for they were built without fortifications. Begin to realize the vast, collective, female organization that the earliest civilizations were built from. The earliest example of writing that has been found is a Temple inventory of goods, grains, livestock, services, and the use of Temple lands from a Temple of the Goddess in what is now Iran. Priestesses developed written language in the service of the Goddess.

Jean—"This is an exercise for the powerful month of Willow:

"Write this incantation on a piece of paper:

> I am Woman and I am Witch. I am Witch and I am Woman. I am the living embodiment on earth of our gracious Lady. When you hear my voice you hear Her words, and when you hear Her words you hear my voice. For I am Witch.

"When you feel the time is right, pronounce the incantation aloud."

Brigid Day (Candlemas, Imbolc, or Festival of Lights) occurs during Willow month. This is a tremendously kinetic time, like life quickening. You may feel as if you've been propelled into sudden, dramatic action. Creative ideas will start to foment, and you'll want to get on with all sorts of projects.

Jessica—"The first Brigid Day celebration I was ever invited to attend was at the house of a new friend when I was living in Montréal. She was from Louisiana, living in town and figuring out where to go from there.

"Gervaise invited everyone she knew to her Candlemas party; my cousin had introduced us, on the premise that we "artistic types" needed to group together. When I arrived at the party, I was presented with a cup of swampwater, a horrid concoction of alcoholic brews native to her hometown, and a small gift from her own personal belongings. Gervaise explained to me that she was opening her life to new possibilities by divesting herself of her old things (including thoughts and ideas) by passing on to her friends old parts of her life. As time went by, Gervaise went on to relocate to London, England, where she became known as a first-class photographer of rock stars and a first-rate photographic teacher. She was also the first visitor to China that I personally knew, when Westerners were just starting to visit."

Helice is the Goddess most associated with Willow; Her name actually refers to the Willow tree. Her priestesses are attached in legend to Mt. Helicon (of Boeotia), where they maintained a shrine. Their work was in the realm of incantation, beneficent or malign. Blessings or curses they dispensed, and were famous, too, for the success of their medicinal herbal magic. Eloquence and poetry fell within their domain, and a certain stream on Helicon was said to confer divinely eloquent inspiration upon men. She is therefore the special patron of poets, and has been ardently adored by practitioners of the mantic arts for centuries on this account.

Imagine that you are walking down a path to a shrine by the side of a river. It is evening; a few stars are showing, the planets Venus and Mars, and a large, gleaming moon is rising. You can hear the nightlife stirring in the reeds and bushes on either side of you. The smell of the river rises on the soft breeze, and the canopy of leaves rustles overhead.

You see the gleam of the river as you approach, and the glow of lanterns in the shrine. Notice the color and features of the small building as you near it and enter. In the center of the enclosure, you see an ancient blackened cauldron. You know that it is filled with the elixir of all life, and that the fluid contents respond, ebb and flow, with the tides of the moon. As you come closer and closer to the life-giving cauldron, look within. What do you see?

Take your vision to keep; it is yours. As you leave the shrine to return to the everyday world, you notice that the cauldron has transformed into a jeweled, silver chalice. You realize that the Grail and the Cauldron are the same thing: the feminine vessel of visions, dreams, nurturing, and life.

Willow

January 31-February 6

8th Day	*Brigantia—the Goddesses of the Underworld stir and awake from their long sleep. Who are they? Can't you feel it? All the goddesses are you.*
9th Day	*With red wine and a soft pillow, open your door to the bride. Repeat three times, "Bride is coming, Bride is here!" And Finally, "Bride is welcome in my home."*
10th Day	*Chinese New Year and Candlemas—meet with a group of women. Each in turn presents what she has created. Become the sponsor of each other's endeavours. Support and protect each other.*
11th Day	*Celebrate Demeter and Persephone's reunion with your mother or daughter. Adopt a witch, Goddesschild or Goddessmother.*
12th Day	*Setsubun Bean Throwing Festival. The beans are your talents. Aim them at fertile ground. The first women's stock brokerage opened in 1870, during this festival. It can work for you too...*
13th Day	*Seek wisdom in water. Gaze into a cup or bowl.*
14th Day	*Aphrodite, Goddess of Love, was born of seafoam, created by tears (water) whipped by action (air), a recipe for love.*

The Priestess of Willow

The Hallows of Willow

Yvonne—"In Willow we change our focus to the alchemy of air and water. The chalice or the athame are the magical tools of this time-frame. It was during the month of Willow, at the outset of my involvement with Jean and Jessica in the writing of this book that I found my current athame.

"Jessica runs a small metaphysical book store in Victoria. From time to time, travellers from exotic places bring her things to sell or trade in the shop, including Tibetan-type ritual objects and symbols. There had been a "Flaming Sword," also called the "Sword of Enlightenment" in the shop for some time, and I really loved it. There came a day, however, when my love of it leaped beyond the passive, detached, appreciative stage, and became a must-have-it kind of thing. Jessica blithely sold it to me at cost, knowing I wouldn't be able to haggle, for reasons of desire as much as tradition (one is not supposed to haggle over the price of magical tools).

"I became the proud owner of this magical thing. It was only later that I found out its specific properties. The Flaming Sword of Enlightenment is for "dispelling the clouds of fear and ignorance," and the proliferation and communication of knowledge and wisdom from the past. It is the best possible guide and protection for an undertaking like the co-authorship of this book. It made me feel that any danger of a backlash of fear or predjudice against witchcraft or Goddess religion that might result was dissipated before it began.

"For the three of us, the impetus to embark on this act of verbal communication was typical of the tone of the post-Brigid Day period. Mental creative activities are favored now, and you may find yourself in a creative foment of ideas. See if it is the mental quickening (blade) or the vessel to contain the idea (the chalice) that finds you now. You will know when you see it. It will have your name on it."

The Cup and the Blade balance each other across the wheel of the year, and across the compass-face of the directions. The Blade symbolizes Air in the East and the Cup symbolizes Water in the West. The Tarot suits of swords and cups conform to these elements. The numerology of the cards give them their specific character and interpretation.

If you think of the sword or blade as a talisman of the left-brain functions and the chalice or cup as a talisman of the right-brain functions, you will be enabled to perform many, potent symbolic acts (or rituals) of personal integration. The conscious, frontal lobe thinking can be wed to the sub-conscious, intuitive capacity in a ritual to effect an inner "Sacred Marriage." Medieval alchemists conceived of this process as a marriage of the lunar consciousness with the solar consciousness, which they personified as the "Goddess" and the "God." Personal sacraments to unite the anima and animus might be construed the same way. In traditional Wiccan ritual the Priestess and Priest effect a symbolic Sacred

Marriage, or "Great Rite," by the device of placing the Blade of Air and Mind within the Chalice of Water and Gnosis (Intuitive, experiential Knowledge).

An understanding of lunar phases is an essential tool of Willow month.

Jessica—"The study of astrology has yielded to me many fascinating insights into numerous facets of human nature over the years. One author whose works I have found very valuable is Mark Robertson, originator of an approach to astrological theory which he calls "Cosmopsychology." The following lunar table is based on his work. The eight lunar phases remind me of our eight "holy days," or Sabbats."

NEW: instinct, projection, spontaneity, (Midwinter)

CRESCENT: a breaking away from the past, the beginnings of productivity (Brigid Day)

FIRST QUARTER: a new start, aggressiveness, the first stirrings of a fight or a time to clear the surroundings to make way for a new order (Spring Equinox)

GIBBOUS: analysis to determine what is needed in order to advance, attention to technique (Beltain)

FULL: receptivity, the need to be flexible and fulfill the structural patterns laid down in the previous phase, the form giving way to content (Midsummer)

DISSEMINATING: fulfillment of purpose, challenging the existing order with creative new beliefs and ideas, decadence (Lammas)

LAST QUARTER: acknowledgement of what has been accomplished and a conscious choice to move toward improvements in the (distant) future (Fall Equinox)

BALSAMIC: release of the old in order to move towards a new vision (Samhain)

February 7-13

15th Day	*Selena, Moon Goddess, brings dreams; record them.*
16th Day	*Start a new dream journal.*
17th Day	*Night of the Dakini Oracle. Examine your passions.*
18th Day	*Can't remember your dreams? Record the colours and emotions.*
19th Day	*Use your library to study colour. The chakra system is a prism.*
20th Day	*White encases you and reflects back emotions sent your way. Witches wear black to attract and absorb energy and information. Try them both.*
21st Day	*During Parentalia Feralia, the Goddesses Vesta and Mania bring peace and love. Enjoy! Wear no pentacles or badges of office. Sign no contract.*

The Hallows of Willow

The Totems of Willow

Women, when living in collective situations, menstruate together like a great, tidal flux. The pygmy women of central Africa, who have in their culture no stigma attached to menstruation or birth whatsoever, menstruate together on or about the full moon. This cycle is fractionally over twenty-eight days in duration and connected intrinsically with the hunting and gathering way of life that they lead. Fertility is never problematic, neither too great nor too slight. The Efi pygmies live in harmony with their environment and have done so for thousands of years. There is no abuse, punishment, or crime in their society. Children are suckled until they no longer seek the breast, and there is no belittlement or verbal abuse of young or old members of the community. This tribal people of Zaïre may be one of the only remaining microcosms of a lifestyle that is harmonious with lunar consciousness and free of shame or stigma regarding womens' cycles. The resultant health of their society is a rare and precious model for the world and our aspirations for health and harmony.

On countless pre-Christian urns and vases from areas of Old Europe (meaning Southeastern Europe and Turkey), the Middle East, Greece, and Crete, there are renderings of the Bee Goddess. This figure is depicted performing tasks or functions that furthered the comfort, prosperity, nourishment and well-being of the community. The ritual life of the Temple complex was seen to provide nurturance on every level, including psychic, emotional, physical, spiritual, and intellectual. The Bee Goddess, bringing food, wine, honey, harp-music, or healing, was a portrayal of the priestesses' functions.

Honey was an important sacred offering, and excavated Temple records show that it figured prominently in the inventory of community wealth. The Bee was regarded as admirable in its thrift and efficiency, industriousness, collective awareness, devoted service to the hive, its infallible finding of sweetness, essence and value, and the purity and beauty of its product. The Bee's natural affinity for color, scent, and flowers was considered a kind of wisdom, and the Bee Goddess is often interchangeable, in Minoan art, with the Butterfly Goddess of transformation. The double-axe symbol of Minoas was called a "Labrys," and was a stylized butterfly, as well as a glyph of the waxing and waning moon—the "Axe That Cuts Both Ways." "Labyrinth" actually means "House of the Double Axe."

Pussy-willows and catkins are often the first nectar-laden blooms to emerge after winter. Their scents awaken the hibernating bees in their hives, and lures them out on their first industrious forays of the Spring.

The activity of bees is directly influenced by the pheromones emitted by the Queen. She is the scource and designer of all of their endeavor. Is it possible that she in turn has a mysterious and as yet little understood response to moon phases?

As a totem of the Goddess, the dove is associated with Aphrodite, Goddess of love, passion, and war. She is also the totem of Astarte, Aphrodite's predecessor, as well as the representative of Sophia, the Gnostic embodiment of Wisdom and the feminine aspect of the Judeo-Christian God.

The ancients considered the human soul feminine in nature, taking the form of a dove after its departure from the body, a belief still perpetuated by the Slavic people. The association of the dove with peace arose from the concept of Aphrodite in her aspect as death-bringer, "Irene," according to one source. However, when one contemplates the possibility of choice inherent in the roles of the Goddess (love, passion, and war), it is feasible to present yet another interpretation: truce, as a prelude to peace.

This is a timely image for the initiation of the partnership model for relationships, especially those between women and men. Truce intimates negotiation, which suggests the equality of the parties involved. The dove's association with the olive, a symbol of Athene (Goddess of wisdom and strategy) shows a co-operation between Aphrodite and Athene, or Love and Wisdom.

The Dove is associated with the number seven: the Pleiades, or Seven Sisters of Greek mythology, were the daughters of Pleione, "Queen of the Sea." Seven was considered to be the number of Sophia; there are seven rays in the system of metaphysics corresponding to seven personality types, and there are seven major energy centers in the body, called "chakras," each concerned with a different area of life as well as a different body organ (corporeal wisdom).

Willow

22nd Day — *Lupercalia—Lupus Diana and Juno Lupa represent natural she-wolf sexual energy. Explore your passions. You can have a vibrant sexual life even if you are celibate. The most important sexual organ is your imagination.*

23rd Day — *You are participating in a rich heritage of women's rituals and traditions, practiced by a very few for two thousand years, ignored by male scholars as obscene and trivial. Always remember—if it is her story it is not considered history.*

24th Day — *Victoria's Day promotes promotions, leadership opportunities and success.*

25th Day — *Sun enters Pisces—Fornacalia asks, "What do you have in the oven?" If you don't turn up the heat, it won't get cooked.*

26th Day — *Spenta Armaiti respects women as cultivators. Cultivate your mind as you would a garden. Remove old dead roots and decayed vegetation.*

27th Day — *Feralia—A purification ritual. It is not wise to live with dead things; let your dead past go. You need space and light for the future.*

28th Day — *Tacita silent averts gossip. Dea Muta—Mother of the Household.*

The Totems of Willow

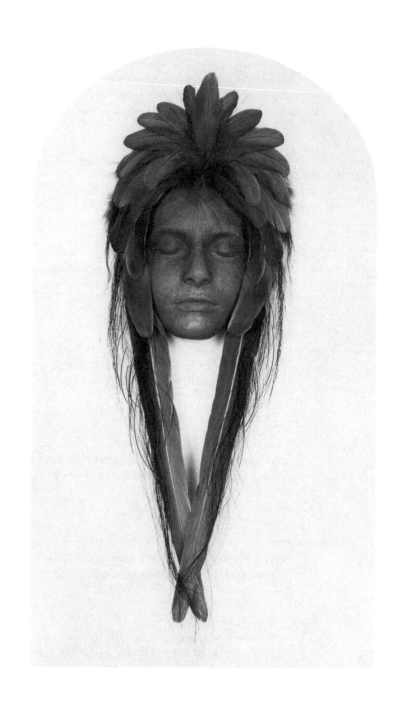

Ash

Ash is in the influence of Pisces. This period is one of the portal-type months. You may experience the sensation of moving into an expanded awareness of the connectedness of your inner world with your outer life. The manner in which you think and dream, your attitudes and expectations, beliefs and biases will yield clear and immediate manifestations to you, through the confluence of the microcosm of the Self with the macrocosm of your environment and relationships.

The Ash tree is the World Tree of myth and legend, the tree of initiation. Odin hung upside down from the giant Ash Yggdrasil—the World Tree of Norse myth—for nine days and nights until he had a mystical revelation of the Runes, regarded as an "oracle" or tool for divination. He hung upside down so as to necessitate an alternative mode of perception, or altered state, one that reversed normal modes. The head (rational linear thought) was upended so that intuition and instinct would be premier. Patience, the attitude of sacrifice, and the willingness to just wait in the place of inaction or enforced helplessness finally bore fruit in the form of Cosmic Realization.

The "Hanged Man" of the Tarot is an archetype of this posture, the upside-down "victim" with one leg straight and the other bent like a crane. The "Hanged Man" card is ruled by the astrological sign of Pisces and has the same passive, sacrificial quality, as a portal to Universal wisdom.

Christianity emerged in the dawn of the Piscean Age with its archetypical sacrificial, Savior god-form. The original emblem of Christianity was the fish. Every astrological influence contains its polarity, so Pisces contains Virgo. The Age of Pisces was therefore influenced by the archetypes of The Fish and The Virgin.

Odin was a Piscean, sacrificial-Savior god-form in Western Europe long before Christianity made its advent there, and the mythopoetic element of Christ's sacrifice on the cross (made of wood, and therefore an acceptable substitute for a Tree) might have paved the way, somewhat, for Christianity's acceptance. There is a hymn, dedicated to the moon, called "Traveller's Prayer" that documents this transposition of symbols. The final verse says:

> In the name of our Lady, bright maiden of grace
> In the name of the King of the City of Peace
> In the name of our Savior, who hung on the Tree
> All Grace to the moon, for eternity.

The "King of the City of Peace" is the Grail King, or Arthur, dwelling in the Glass Castle in the central circle of the Celtic tri-cosmos, Annwn—a place of rest and tranquility associated with Glastonbury. The Savior who hung from the Tree is very obviously Odin, and this "hymn" shows just one of the ways that the Bardic branch of the Druids kept The Mystery Tradition alive, under the guise of conventional, Christian piousness. This would not have been too difficult, as the Christ figure in many ways resembled Odin, although he very much resembled another of his predecessors, Mithras, as well.

This month concludes with the Spring Equinox, or Eostre (from which we get "Easter"), from Astara (Astarte, Ishtar). The Celtic name for the Vernal Equinox was "Alban Eiler." This holy day commemorated the appearance of the morning star (Venus/Ishtar) on the horizon in the Spring. The resurrection festival of Osiris was a similar rite. The ancient Egyptian Piscean-sacrificial god-form, Osiris, was dismembered by brother Set, then his members were retrieved and re-integrated by Isis—all except for the phallus, which was eaten by a fish. The festival was characterized by the eating of dried fish, a custom followed by Christian Copts in Egypt, upon the festival of Easter, to this day.

The dismemberment theme is common to all shamanic intitiations and is part of the mystical death/rebirth scenario. It is the stage prior to re-memberment, or psychological integration. But the dismemberment sacrifice of the Ash-Piscean initiation is qualified by a focus upon the phallus and castration. In some versions of the myth, the Meliai (Ash spirits) sprang from the blood of Ouranos when Cronos castrated him. (By other, more authentic accounts they were Ash Tree Dryads who dwelt at the root of the World Tree, like the Three Fates, or Norns.) The god, Attis, was said to have been struck by ecstatic madness by his mother, Cybele, when he strayed to love a nymph or dryad. This madness is said to have caused him to castrate himself, then hang himself from a tree. Priests of Cybel in Rome, who had to "become as women" to serve Cybele in the temple, did castrate themselves in self-mutilation initiatory frenzies during the festival of the God—where we now observe Easter, near to the Spring Equinox. (The date in the first century BCE was March 25th.) After this induction, the priests wore women's clothing, jewelry, and cosmetics. It is important to note that this is how the Goddess Cybel was worshipped during Patriarchy, in Imperial Rome. The phallus is equated with left-brain, conscious thinking, and "The Word."

The Ash tree is sacred to Poseidon, God of the Sea. Staves or talismans made of Ash were once thought to prevent drowning.

The Rune for Ash is Naudhiz. Naudhiz is a rune of struggle, strain, necessary action against restraint or stagnation. It is a shamanic rune.

The Gaelic name for Ash is Nuin, its letter is N, and the Ogham symbol is shown below.

Rune
Naudhiz

Ogham
Nuin

Ash

February 21-27

1st Day	*With Ash the light returns, bringing a rebirth of the lunar spirit—wiser and stronger, reaching for the light of new opportunity and challenge.*
2nd Day	*Concordia—a time to make peace within the family.*
3rd Day	*Terminalia—after peace comes a need to set boundaries. Good fences make good friends.*
4th Day	*Regifugium—the king hides, for it is time to die—a sacrifice to save his people, a fool befuddled by the attention takes his place and dies as proxy. An unworthy sacrifice? King or fool? Your choice.*
5th Day	*If you sacrificed the king, the Egyptian Goddess, Nut, brings you healing, for death is not the end of things.*
6th Day	*With Hygieia's wisdom, learn the messages of illness so as to avoid having to have them.*
7th Day	*Do not ignore the crone for her wisdom is seeing and recording.*

The Ash Tree

The Priestess of Ash

Imagine this scenario: You are the holder of the sacred chalice, in the glass castle, in the heart of the wood. Inside this cup you hold there is a precious gift for someone for it is the cup of life, but they must be able and willing to find you, and drink of the cup, to receive the elixir. Imagine that weeks, months, even years have gone by, and still you wait for the seeker. You begin to draw the seeker toward you. Gradually, you begin to get a sense of the seeker's approach. One day, you can actually see this person in the distance, through the glass walls of your castle. As she or he gets closer, you begin to make out the seeker's identity. Is it someone you know? Is it a stranger? Is it yourself, or a part of yourself?

Allow the seeker to come closer and closer. Eventually, this person is standing directly before you, clear and distinct. Bless the contents of the Chalice, and allow the Seeker to drink from it. Let the scene fade from view.

Now, imagine the scene again, only now you are the seeker, at the fringes of the wood. You know that the Grail Castle is in there, somewhere, and that you must find it—to drink the cup of enlightenment. See yourself venturing into the forest; you may have to cut your way through the undergrowth with your sword. There are towering trees on every side, and a tangle of brush on the forest floor. Eventually you see the Glass Castle glinting in the distance, on a rise in the middle of a clearing. You see that there is a moat, with a bridge that you must cross to go inside the glass walls. After you do this, you travel down many corridors, penetrating to the very heart of the castle. You enter a glass chamber. Here there stands a figure holding the sacred chalice. As you approach the figure, you see more and more clearly who it is. When you have come close enough to the person to stand directly opposite, regard the figure, and notice every detail of his or her appearance. At a certain moment, this person will offer you the cup from which to drink. As you drink, imagine that strength, vision, clarity, and enlightenment are pouring into you. Feel the magical liquid as it flows down your throat.

Afterward, let the image fade, but keep the magical, rejeuvenating effects.

The "Meliae" are Ash tree nymphs, or dryads. They are a version of the Moerae, or Fates. They are wither triform, meaning a triple divinity, or nine-fold—like the nine Muses. The sacred number Nine, connoting completion and the kind of finality associated with the Fates, triples this triplicate. This is like an increased octave of the creative power of Three, and a very ancient expression of the Triple Goddess.

A pictograph dating from the Paleolithic depicts the Nine Clan Mothers. They stand in a row, bare-breasted, wearing bell skirts. The first three have white skirts, and are spinning a coil of yarn-like energy. The second group of three are garbed in red and weave the yarn into a pattern. The final three wear black and are the Crones who cut the coil, severing the life-line. The young God, a form of Mercury of Hermes, reels before them as if in a swoon. A tiny replica of him bounds away in the background on the flank of a stag, an image of the young God's oracular trance journey, spun and facilitated by the Nine Clan Mothers.

This idea is at the root of the Nine Muses, the Nine Priestesses of the Isle of Women, the Nine Fairies of Avalon, the Nine Maidens of the standing stones, and many other mythic groupings of nine. The Magdalenian Triple Goddess is their direct ancestress.

Odin is the God of Ash. When it is said that Odin hung for nine nights upon the sacred Ash (the World Tree) what is meant is that he accessed the primordial, feminine wisdom of the Meliae, becoming all-wise. Odin is also Wotan, or Wodan, and corrolated to Mercury. His day is Wednesday (Woden's day) or French Mercredi. Wednesday is therefore Ash day, and "Ash Wednesday" occurs during this month.

The qualities of Ash confer the ability to translate understanding between the various realms of existence. This is a quality special to Mercury/Wotan and, like the fishes of Pisces swimming in both directions, creates a synergy of opposites. This is another aspect of the dynamic dualism of Pisces that colors the experience of Ash month. All things contain the shadow of their opposite within them, and Pisces contains the qualitites of Virgo, which opposes Pisces across the wheel of the year. Ash month is influenced by the archetypes of The Fish and The Virgin, therefore, and the Age of Pisces saw the advent of Christianity with its original emblem of the fish and the myth of the Virgin Mother. A medieval ballad sings of "The little fish that the Virgin found in the well," referring no doubt to Mary and Christ, but also to an iconography much older. A later Celtic form of Odin/Wotan/Mercury was Gwydion—a sea god who could shape-shift into the form of a fish.

The mutually creative interpenetration of the inner and the outer, the conscious and subconscious realms of Self is the power of Ash. Surrender is required, a relaxing of the managing ego, a reversal of the controlling intellect. Psychic sensitivity and intuitive gifts are the fruits of patience. Humility is required in order to let go of conscious management and control and wait in the place of inaction. This can feel like helplessness, but it is not. It is simply a refraining from noise and activity so as to allow the subtler energies their range of expression. Waiting and watching, it will become obvious how your inner life affects manifestation in the outer world. And your quiet attention to the sounds your soul makes will be repaid to you as a clearly heard message, like an oracle from your own, deep understanding.

Ash

8th Day	*Plant your seeds in Zamyaz — Mother Earth.*
9th Day	*Matronalia — Juno Lucina, Protector of women, bestows her power upon you.*
10th Day	*Vesta tells us that all gracious loving acts are sacred to her; to each their own preference in devotional matters.*
11th Day	*Buy a small doll in a hobby shop and dress her as your favourite goddess.*
12th Day	*As you set your table you also set an altar—place settings in four directions so fire, water, earth and air are all represented. Each meal is a ceremony to one or more goddess(es). Flora and Hecate are honored today.*
13th Day	*Isis and Aphrodite grace your mirrors and "vanity" tables. These too are altars.*
14th Day	*Celtic time of flowering — search for small unfolding buds in garden or park. Place on mantle or bookshelf. Yes, they are altars also.*

The Priestess of Ash

The Hallows of Ash

Yvonne—"The way in which the chalice and the blade interact is so very fascinating. As I have mentioned, my wand is a very watery kind of wand, being made of Hazel wood, the water-diviner. Another reason my wand is so watery, going like an arrow for essence and meaning (the content of the cup), is because it is shaped like a blade. The incisive action of the truth-seeking sword is as if magnetized to the blessings of the cup, that 'encompasseth all understanding.'

"There is an electro-magnetic response, on the part of water, to light. Nucleic acids suspended in water linked to form molecular chains, which formed the basis for life on earth, in response to light. Light cuts through the translucent, magnetic water like quicksilver, or consciousness, and the water responds by reconfiguring its energy and uncasing new forms.

"The two elements, air and water, are constantly engaged in the dynamic of their polarity. The mental faculties of analysis and exposition, intellect and focus, are constantly interacting with the intuitive faculties of emotion, desire, imagination, fantasy, and creativity. Logic probes dreams and visions and yields revelation and understanding. Dreams and visions wait for the one-point focus of conscious awareness so that they may flower into new responses.

"The symbol of the clear-edged blade of conscious mind wedded to the fertile, magnetic intuitive sense is the image of the blade within the cup. This image has so much more to it than the mere significance of phallic penetration that I've heard attributed. That is to reduce the significance to a trivialization, because the symbology is really about aspects of consciousness in a dynamic relationship. It may well be that the dynamic of sexual interaction mirrors this alchemy, but that is as it should be, as the entire Universe, whether it is observed in microcosm or macrocosm, is constantly engaged in this dynamic of self-penetration and self-creation."

Jean—"It was time, the Elders said, to find my blade; I had avoided it far too long. A knife, to me, was used to make a sandwich or cut flowers. Occasionally, I used one to cut a circle. [Ritually—see Appendix A.] The idea of carrying a knife, the symbol of my solar or masculine energy, was disturbing to me. Finally I asked for advice.

"'Go back to your beginnings,' the Elders suggested.

"A cedar chest belonging to my grandfather was the clue to my past. A blue velvet box containing a child's knife, fork and spoon lay on top. Above my initials on each handle, a smiling 'Little Red Riding Hood' carried a basket on her left arm, and her right hand rested on a friendly-looking wolf. One prong of the fork was twisted; I had used it to try to pry apart the dining-room table. The bowl of the spoon was nicked and scarred by tiny teeth. The knife was perfect— bright, shiny, and unused. Obviously, as a child, I considered knives to be purely ornamental.

"The message became even more clear, for beside the knife, fork and spoon—wrapped in tissue paper—was a beautiful, pearl-handled, Victorian fish knife. The blade was engraved with sea shells and waterlilies. I had found my blade. Later, I placed it on the altar and dedicated it to Her service. As Merikat bent to bind it to my waist with a black cord, I noticed a strange twist to her lips. Was it envy, annoyance, or amusement?

"'Please let it be annoyance,' I prayed to the Goddess. I couldn't bear it to be amusement. I was only sixteen.

"Over the next decades, a theatrical, jeweled dagger from a production of Hamlet joined the fish knife. A very proper black-handled athame and its white-handled twin, the blades symbolically engraved, found their way to the altar. Inherited blades and gifts were received, and later found their way to new homes and owners.

"The time came when I needed to make drastic changes in my life. I needed to find my solar or masculine energy, for I would have to be both father and mother to my family. The lunar, silver knife that had served my frivolous lifestyle was no longer suitable. A box in a thrift shop caught my attention. It contained an old knife; the cracked handle was held together by string and the blade was discoloured and pitted.

"'Go back to your beginnings,' the words echoed in my head, and suddenly I was a small child sitting in the bottom of a canoe. The inside was shiny with varnish and I was admiring my scarred knees, when a large silver fish fell from the sky—or, at least, that's how it seemed to me. The fish lurched, twisted and gasped in the air. Suddenly, two large, tanned hands removed the hook and, with a knife, killed the fish and removed the flesh from the bones. In what seemed like a few seconds the flesh was sizzling in a pan over a campfire and the rest of the fish was placed on a rock at the edge of the water, to provide a meal for the gulls. Soon I was handed a plate of fish.

"'Eat it,' I was told, 'You like fish.'

"I had eaten fish before, but I had never known that something was killed to provide us with food. I paid a quarter for the knife, and as I walked home, I knew I would sever my links with the past, take all the love, care, and tenderness—like the flesh of the fish—to nourish me. The rest I would leave behind. Perhaps it would sustain someone else with different needs or tastes.

"The two fish knives grace my altar, one silver and elegant with lunar energy, the other strong and sharp with solar power. In this lifetime, I was born in March, my sign two fish swimming in opposite directions. And I never eat fish..."

Ash

15th Day	*Mother and daughters — this relationship was chosen by you prior to birth. Why did you need to be linked to this person? Make some kind of contact.*
16th Day	*On this International Women's Day, Chinese women celebrate Mother Earth's birthday. Make a difference.*
17th Day	*Aphrodite and Adonis share a day devoted to male and female beauty. We celebrate the beauty that is you.*
18th Day	*Hypalia was called the Divine Pagan by the Christian clergy that caused her to be slashed to death by sea shells. Her crime? She taught men.*
19th Day	*Why did they choose sea shells?*
20th Day	*As we come to the equinox, a time of balance, light and dark, solar lunar equally — joy and fear combine.*
21th Day	*You can not stop the tide or rule the wind. The goddess chant begins "Oh she will bring the buds of spring, and laugh among the flowers."*

The Hallows of Ash

The Totem of Ash

The dolphin has been revered as a type of demi-god of the sea by many cultures. A mystical relationship with dolphins is claimed by a good many people. Dolphins are connected with the lost world of Atlantis and with the quality of expanded consciousness. Also, compassion, Agape, sophistication, telepathy, gentleness and evolvement are associated with these gentle creatures. Dolphins have a long-suffering, sacrificial air. It's as if they have been waiting for hundreds of years for us to get smart enough to stop poisoning the oceans so that we can all have some hope for survival, but they'll still love us, even if we fail miserably. They'll be one of the first species to go, of course, but that's all right. They are eternally forgiving and accepting, and nothing shakes their pure, unconditional compassion.

Dolphin herds are attributed with the rescue of downed sailors, floundering divers, and swimmers in extremity. This savior-like quality is legendary. They were a favorite subject of Minoan fresco artists, sculptors, metal workers, and potters. Currently, they are a favorite subject of the New Age in the roles of, alternately, post-Atlantean messengers or extra-terrestrial messengers. They still evoke that quality of compassionate intervention for us, as if they will sacrifice themselves willingly so that we may gain enlightenment and be saved at the last minute from destruction (by their friends, who are either extra-terrestrials, or Atlanteans, depending on the version you prefer).

The character of the dolphin is like the Ash Tree in the ability to bear your difficulty or enforced inaction. Like the giant Ash tree, Dolphin will support your process as you approach understanding — unfailingly and with boundless endurance and good grace. Dolphin will even be self-sacrificing, if that is required. You can send Dolphin on what might seem like a suicide mission into the depths of your own psyche, to retrieve wisdom. The Dolphin will be willing, compassionate, and helpful.

Imagine that you are standing on a high, windy cliff. It is the Spring of the year, and a mild breeze ruffles your hair and loose garments. It is warm, and the sea below is calm and clear. The sea calls to you to dive to its depths, and because this is a waking dream, you do so. Feel yourself arc far out over the water in a powerful, flying dive. Now feel yourself enter the water, the clear substance of it closing over your body as you dive deep into the blue-green darkness. You find that you can see and breathe, effortlessly, underwater. You see Dolphin swimming up to meet you, his form growing more distinct as he approaches. As he swims into focus, you reach out to take a hold of his dorsal fin, and he carries you with him through the water, swiftly and gracefully. As you and Dolphin cruise through the depths, notice the underwater terrain. Notice the abundant life in the fertile, aquatic realm. Dolphin dives deeper and deeper until you are skimming over the ocean floor like a fleeting shadow.

Dolphin takes you to the mouth of an underwater grotto. You enter and regard a room of ancient treasure. What do you see? Is any of it yours? There is something here that belongs to you, from the past... a gift, a talent, some essential property of yours. Reclaim it. Bring it with you as you leave the grotto to rejoin Dolphin. Dolphin takes you on a tour of an entire, underwater realm of possibility. Enjoy this journey for as long as you wish.

Dolphin begins to rise again to the surface. He brings you to a sheltered beach, where you awaken from your travels, as if from a dream. Dolphin says, "If ever you have need of me, in realm of dreams or of the sea, call me and I will come to your aid, for your quest is worthy."

Ash month is sacred to Poseidon, whose sea chariot is drawn by dolphins (or by horses). Poseidon's earliest form was the feminine Posidieja, a Minoan Sea Goddess. Cretan funeral urns (shaped like wombs) displayed Dolphins, representative of the soul's journey to other realms. Another name for the Sea Goddess, "Delphine," means both "womb," and "dolphin." Delphine also assumed Mermaid form. The first Priestess of the oracular shrine, Delphi (womb), was called Delphine.

Ash

22nd Day — *Ua Zit, The Snake Goddess, teaches us to ward off poverty with the wisdom of her servant, the snake. Make wisdom your servant and partner.*

23rd Day — *As Hilaria begins, celebrate the goddess-given gifts of wit, theatre and comedy.*

24th Day — *Examine both your friendship braid, for new additions and removals, and your cobwebs for progress.*

25th Day — *Liberia. Drink the juice of the grape in honor of Bacchus.*

26th Day — *Sheela Na Gig in early Christian churches, grimacing, squatting figures of contorted women with genitals exposed. Who are they and what fears or expectations do they signify? Find a picture of Judy Chicago's "Dinner Party."*

27th Day — *Quintaria—five-day feast of Athena. Treat yourself and friends to music, food and theatre as Ash ends in joy.*

28th Day — *Frigga celebrates women's right to be vulgar. Find the word in a dictionary.*

The Totem of Ash

Hawthorn

The Hawthorn tree is significant of cleansing, purity, and chastity. The type of "chastity" that Hawthorn suggests is not mere sexual abstention. It is more a type of sovereignty over yourself, in as much as you exist in your own right, for your own purposes, and are not appropriated or distorted by anyone else's agenda. Of course, this often includes a period of celibacy, as sexual connection establishes an energetic bond that is visible to some as a bridge, or arc, of light, and so compromises the purely sovereign state of selfhood to a degree. Perhaps this is the underlying reason for the valuing of abstention during some periods of personal retreat or clearing.

The word "Virgin" originally meant, simply, "unmarried," and had nothing to do with the concept of an unbreached maidenhead. "Virgin" priestesses, therefore, were active in the tendering of sexual sacraments to the Great Goddess, without any conflict between their sexuality and their Virgin status. This simply meant that they were obligated to no one and no thing, other than their own spiritual evolution within the life of the Temple. They were not responsible for, beholden to, or owned and ruled by a husband and his estate, but were free women.

In the "Golden Age" of patriarchal Greece, vestiges of this tradition remained in the custom of "free women," meaning unmarried courtesans, who held court in intellectual and artistic circles of the urban centers. These women, unconstrained by the rigid conduct codes that affected married women, were free to be visible on the city streets, to live independently and very comfortably, dispensing ancient knowledge and philosophical acumen in the salons, colleges, and schools that centered around them. Aristotle's "master" was one of these women.

Sappho, living perhaps two hundred years earlier than this period, at the onset of the "Golden Age" (or solar-god stage), in the island sanctuary of Lesbos and called "the first poet" in the formal, classical sense, was a "free woman." She never married. She had many pupils and consorts, and was respected for her mastery of song, dance, sexual arts, ritual worship, philosophy, music, and languages. Her poems often incorporated multi-level puns, with double meanings in several languages simultaneously. Noble families sent their offspring to study with her in order that they absorb the cultural heritage of the Age. But her lifetime came just at the brink of the dangerous loss of status that these virgin, philosopher priestesses suffered. Most of her prolific body of work was purposely destroyed, with only fragments surviving to be painstakingly pieced together by Victorian archeologists over two thousand years later. In her role as sexual healer and teacher, artist, musician, philosopher, and spiritual leader, Sappho was the ideological descendant of thousands of years of the tradition of such women— called "quadisha," "hetaera," or "hierodule," meaning "Holy Woman."

Knowing that the word Virgin was understood in this sense in the ancient world, it is possible to look at the legend of Christ in a different light. Mary was not married at the time that she conceived. She was, therefore, a Virgin.

This is the sense of the word we think of when we speak of a Virgin forest, or Virgin land... wild, uncompromised, existing on its own terms, in its own right, for its own purposes, with no liens or tenders on the life that thrives within. This is the type of chastity invoked by Hawthorn, and as such, offers potent protection. Hawthorn trees were planted as a hedge, or barrier, to intrusion. Their thorns protected the core from unwanted, invading influences, and guarded the integrity of the interior space.

Jessica—"Thorn, specifically, Hawthorn (or Whitethorn or May) to which Blackthorn is related, was used by the Greeks and Romans in nuptial rites, being sacred to Hymen, a god of marriage. Leaves of the tree were scattered about the bridal chamber 'to promote chastity' but if one examines Thorn's function as a protector of sacred space, it is easy to see this ancient custom in a new light. Any work which promotes the alchemical process of solar/lunar integration (i.e., the union of the masculine and the feminine aspects of the individual) would be under the auspices of Thorn. Thus it is clear that any enactment of the Sacred Marriage (hieros gamos) would be associated with Thorn. Hawthorn is also associated with cleansing and clearing.

"During this month it was customary for our ancestors to wear old clothes, cover their bodies with ashes, abstain from sexual activity and clean house. We have inherited the concept of 'spring cleaning' from this custom. This month of fasting, cleaning and abstention was forerunner to the festival of Beltane, during which one could expect the conception of children to occur. Having prepared the body with fasting and cleansing, people were thus able to give any child conceived a hallowed (literally, 'made holy' or whole) condition in which to grow."

The sun moves into the sign of Aries just at the outset of Hawthorn, and the Vernal Equinox occurs here, too. At the Equinox (Alban Eiler) there is a balance of the light and dark portions of the twenty-four hour cycle. The solar and lunar influences are thought to be equal.

The Hawthorn Rune is Hagalaz, which signifies sudden occurences, impartiality, the seed stirring within the soil in the spring. This is the Mother Rune from which all others evolved.

The Gaelic name for Hawthorn is Huathe, the letter is H, and the Ogham symbol is shown below.

Rune
Hagalaz

Ogham
Huathe

Hawthorn

1st Day	*Spring equinox, perfect balance of light and dark, solar and lunar energy. Celebrate Persephone's return from the underworld and Demeter's joy.*
2nd Day	*Spring seedtime. She awakens and the rainbow is her sign. Search for your own rainbow.*
3rd Day	*Minerva bids you, "Be joyful." In your joy you do not forget the cold of winter and the promises you made yourself.*
4th Day	*Fast in the morning and feast in the evening.*
5th Day	*On Lady Day, she is poised for spring. The powerful goddess images of the dreamtime are replaced by the warm comfort of the Lady. We part and end encounters with a gentle wish... "Lady Bless."*
6th Day	*Fercula. It is unwise to strike the earth with iron before the sixth of Hawthorn. The armed invasions of the iron age were inimicable to fairies (witches).*
7th Day	*Consult your psychic-self. If you haven't found your tools, begin in earnest. We recommend the tarot...*

The Hawthorn Tree

The Priestess of Hawthorn

The priestess of Hawthorn is both the virgin spring, unsullied and untrammelled—and its protector. In this relationship, you are both the zealously guarded, pure, wild essence, and the thorns that prevail against invasion. During this period, you might consider a spiritual retreat, a fast, or cleansing diet. Regard yourself as perfect and immaculate in your essential Self, in your conception of yourself, and then adopt a stance of fierce resolve to defend this purity—your natural condition.

You may want to look back over your life, starting with your earliest memories. Recall the first time when you might have been terribly upset, or a time when you were suffering. Look to see if there is a sense of injustice connected with this memory; have you been wronged or misjudged in some way? Has a parent or a teacher projected an erroneous or distorted image on to you? If so, go back into the scene in a visualization, and defend youself. You can see yourself saying or doing the things you were unable or too small to say or do at the time. Or you can see yourself enter the scene as your adult self, defending, protecting and comforting your child self.

This type of visualization is so powerful that it actually changes the past, or what we might call the "Roots of Karma," and puts your present and your future on a different and firmer foundation. This is due to the fact that, having re-visioned (revised) the scene or scenes that damaged your sense of Self in the past, you have supplied yourself with an advocate, even if it is your own, present, grown-up self doing the advocacy. If the visualization is powerful, it will go deep to subconscious areas of your psyche. In other words, if your light Alpha-trance is convincing (and they always are—this is our "deep" mind, and it is programmed in precisely this manner), your memory of the events that have harmed your self-esteem and your sense of yourself will transform, and likewise your present and ongoing reality, for you will remember having been protected and respected, instead of having been defamed. You will, thereafter, think of yourself as someone who is worthy of protection and respect, and this will change your life accordingly.

This is also a month that may inspire you to clean house, literally as well as figuratively. Clearing out emotional baggage is often helped along by a thorough house-cleaning, disgarding old, burdened memories and restoring your environment to its prime condition.

Hawthorn leads up to Oak month, during which Beltane, or May Day, occurs. This a good time to take stock spiritually and review your decision to embrace the Craft of the Wise. It is also an ideal time to perform a self-dedication —to declare your affinities with Craft emblems and beliefs. In a "dedication," you would acknowledge and avow patron God or Goddess-forms, and pledge your talents, strengths and abilities to the service of Craft principles. Or you would simply declare yourself a Priestess of the Craft, an act of self-recognition prior to self-initiation.

The following story relates the tale of a Priestess whose self-dedication brought her into contact with an ancient and numinous deity of the Craft, the Great Stag. The Stag is a totem of Hawthorn month.

Jessica—"I once had a friend with whom I shared a mutual admiration. She has since moved away and we have lost touch these last few years. She was instrumental in bringing feminine awareness to many people in her community. I wish her well.

"One day we were conversing, becoming better acquainted with each other and she told me her story about her decision to embrace the Craft. She and her husband lived in a beautiful, well-equiped rural home surrounded by wildlife. Being a 'city girl' like myself, this had been her first-hand introduction to the natural world.

"The evening of her dedication (her acknowledgement of her Priestess self), she decided to enact her ritual out-of-doors and "sky-clad." As evening turned to night she bathed, went outside, removed her robe, and began her salutation and invocation. Suddenly she heard a man's footsteps nearby.

"Siezed by a sense of panic, she ran back to her house and into her husband's arms. Concern quickly drew them both to the window to see who the intruder could be. Instead of a man, they saw the form of a great stag in the moonlight, heading back into the woods.

"'Some Priestess,' she said to me, summing up the story. 'Some Priestess.'"

Hawthorn

March 28-April 3

8th Day	*In the name of Kwan Yin, be merciful in all your dealings today.*
9th Day	*As Diana, prepare for coming renewal of virginity and the need to hunt.*
10th Day	*Prepare for "Feast of Green." Before the "April Fool," there was the "Green Man," lover/consort of the Green Earth.*
11th Day	*Kindness paid to strangers reaps its own reward. Toast the kindly ones, repay with loving actions.*
12th Day	*Bathe and dress Venus in her most becoming robe. Who is Venus? You are.*
13th Day	*Feast of A-Ma, Portugese goddess/patron of fishing folk.*
14th Day	*Cerealia—seeedtime. Celebrate with Demeter by choosing and nourishing your most beautiful and fertile seed thoughts.*

The Priestess of Hawthorn

The Hallows of Hawthorn

There are ancient, Celtic images connected with the month of Hawthorn. For one thing, this is the month that leads up to Oak month. After Oak month, the tone of the season changes, with efforts bearing fruitful, visible issue. Hawthorn is like a preparatory period of waiting, so as to be in readiness for fecundation and harvest.

Merlin met his "Nemesis," in the form of Nimue, in a clearing surrounded by Hawthorn. This is an example of the idea of Hawthorn encircling and protecting sacred or magical space. Nimue is the Celtic name for the Aegean Goddess, Nemesis. Nemesis is one of the three Fates, a later version of the Archaic Greek triple Goddess conforming to the triple Goddess, Fata Morgana; and her role is to provide feminine balance to the male—and sometimes to check overweening growth or expansion out of balance and proportion. The Fata Morgana is also called The Morrigan (or Battle Crow), and Her three aspects are Nimue, Elaine, and Morgan La Fey (or Magda, or Mabd). These aspects are the maiden, mother, and crone phases of a single archetype, much as the new, full, and waning moon are all phases of the same cosmic body.

When Merlin met with Nimue in the Hawthorn grove, it represented a negotiation between the male and female magical principles within sacred space. They met there to contract for teaching or healing, or for the transmission of magical lore. Their final meeting resulted in Nimue enclosing Merlin (a specific, Druidic type of wisdom) in the Crystal Cave (underground, esoteric, protected place) until the time was right for him to re-emerge (or until the world was again safe for earth-spirituality and natural magic).

From the same body of myth and lore, the story of King Arthur and Excalibur incorporates the male and female principles in the imagery of the magical sword, Excalibur, and the Lady of the Lake, Elaine. Nimue is also associated with the Lady of the Lake, as the young, questing aspect, or acolyte. The Lady of the Lake is both the lake (or water) itself, and the spirit and consciousness of water.

Arthur had been instructed by Merlin in the ways of magic while he was still a boy. He knew all about the wisdom and secret lore of the Lady of the Lake, and was an initiate into Her mysteries. Years later, the dying King Arthur sends Sir Bidevere to return the magical male principle, the sword Excalibur, to the Goddess so that its immense power doesn't fall into the wrong hands. When Bidevere arrives at the mystical lake, where the magical Isle of Avalon is floating in the mists at the center, he finds that he cannot bring himself to throw away the sword. When he returns, feigning having done so, Arthur asks him what he saw when he threw Excalibur into the lake. Sir Bidevere replied that he saw only the waves upon the water, whereupon Arthur knew that he was lying, and sent him off again, with the injunction to do it right this time.

Bidevere returns to the lake, and sadly throws the magnificent Excalibur into the water, only to see a hand emerge from the waves to seize the sword, followed by the beautiful Lady of the Lake, who then takes the sword back down into the depths. When he reports this miraculous vision to Arthur, Arthur knows that the power of the sword has been safely restored to the Goddess, and all is well. The Lady of the Lake is Elaine, and also Nimue and Morgan La Fey. In some versions of the tale, Nimue has a fish-tail and is associated with the moon.

The spiritual and sexual alchemy of air (symbolized by the sword, Excalibur) and water (symbolized by Elaine, the Lady of the Lake—bearer of the cup) is beautifully shown in these tales. There is a reverential quality to the surrender of the sword to the lake, and an understanding of the importance of wedding heart to mind, and feelings to intellect.

Hawthorn

15th Day	*Megalesia, when men castrated themselves to be like Attis. In reality they feared loss of power at Beltane. Will you aid, condone, or prevent? The power is yours for the lunar season has begun.*
16th Day	*Fortuna, Day of Fate and Fortune. Will you recognize your opportunities?*
17th Day	*Stretch and feel your emerging strength.*
18th Day	*Blajini—Rule with kindness.*
19th Day	*Make or purchase crescent-shaped cookies to share at Diana's bow—the crescent moon.*
20th Day	*Hocktide—Saxon women defeated the Danes after the male army fled in fear. Wear red in honour of the leader, Rheada.*
21st Day	*Gaia, the earth, is pregnant. Share her joy.*

The Hallows of Hawthorn

The Totems of Hawthorn

King Arthur is associated with the white stag, appearing at the edge of the Hawthorn-encircled clearing in the forest. Whenever the sacred marriage, or male/female alchemy, of intellect and feeling, mind and intuition is about to take place, the stag will appear. In the body, air is associated with the mental functions, occurring all over the body, but especially associated with areas from the center of the chest to the crown of the head. Water is associated with the bowl of the belly. Here, fertile creativity, astral communication, intuition, and the moon-ruled navel chakra are emphasized. When these centers come into communication with each other, the sacred marriage is taking place. This wholeness and integrity is what the white stag heralds.

The Unicorn was symbolic of virginal purity in Medieval mysticism, and also of innocent, unihibited eroticism. Wild and untamable, the Unicorn would become gentle and lay his phallic, DNA-spiral, rainbow-hued horn in the lap of a "virgin." Often, the virginal, Goddess-like maiden is depicted in the medieval tapestries in a springtime garden, with the Unicorn on one side, and the stag on the other. To the mystical, medieval mind, this tableau presented an entire array of meanings. The underground survival of pagan beliefs within Christian mysticism was kept alive by the subversive activity of the Troubadours, the guild of story-tellers and songsters who were the ideological descendants of the Druidic Bards. The songs and tales, carried from town to town, castle to castle, by the Troubadours, were filled with ancient, Pagan imagery and Druidic lore. Couched in Christian sentiment, symbols of wild untrammelled eroticism (the Stag and the Unicorn) dallied with maidens in the Hawthorn glade. Imagine yourself, watched over by the Stag, meeting with the Unicorn in the Hawthorn-protected sanctity of the forest.

Herne The Hunter is an aspect of Cernunnos, the antlered God. This entity has been a feature of the Old Religion since the dawn of human history, when His image was inscribed on rocks and cavern walls. The archetype of valor, life/death, and sacrifice, Herne is the Hunter who is also the Hunted. This empathetic dynamic describes the human trait of identifying with one's prey. The objectified consciousness of humaness means that it is impossible to hunt and kill any living thing without being doomed to imagine, only too clearly, what it is like to be hunted and killed. Thus the death/sacrifice is experienced by the perpetrator as well, vicariously. The consciousness of being, also, prey for the sustenance of other life-forms is endemic to the Craft—to know oneself as an integral part of the food chain, a part of the All Being who continually consumes itself in order to create itself. The Herne archetype is the sacred realization of symbiosis with all life/death. He makes us aware of the gift of life and sustenance, and that sacrifice is always inherent within it.

This is the type of awareness that formed a sacred bond with other forms of existence, animal or vegetable. The creature who gave its life that we may live was considered humane and divine. The grain that forfeited its life to our nurturance was no less an animate participant in the round of Life/Death, and was called "The Green Man," "John Barleycorn," "The Corn King," "The Year King," and other names. His archetype was the original model of Attis, Tammuz, Damuzi, Adonis, Mithras, and Christ, among others—the Divine Son type Godforms who gave their lives that we may live, in the here and now or the afterlife, whichever was valued more by the current culture. Even now, Christian mysticism identifies the Stag with Christ (the Hart in the Wood) but the Stag as sacrificial savior God is older than Christianity by millenia.

Jean—"The Great Stag, aloof and mysterious, seen in fleeting glimpses on far-off hilltops or stalking with measured tread across green meadows...

"Dancers, with arms raised above their heads to symbolize His horns and feet flashing in complicated patterns to mirror His progression through woodland paths... Hunters sometimes found on the forest floor the bodies of two stags, their horns locked together in battle, dead of wounds and starvation, the victor and the defeated locked in a deadly embrace... This image became a symbol of the futility of War.

"Still, the Great Stag was seen alone, serene, the benevolent God/King of the forest. The Celts knew Him as Cernunnos—masculine sexuality, wisdom and nobility at its finest. He has retained respect, though He is remembered and honored today only by a few of the traditional witches. Misunderstood and diminished by our enemies, the Stag was replaced by a domestic goat. Many groups accepted this substitute, influenced by the goat's ready availability and the propaganda of our detractors. Easy to parody, the goat replaced the noble Stag.

"As Herne, a hunter condemned to wear the head and antlers of a sacred Stag killed in a holy grove, he haunted the dreams of men. Herne the Hunter and the Wild Hunt sweep across the countryside each autumn. His portrait, framed in Oak leaves, reaches us across the centuries to remind us of this noble being. The wild cries and the pounding hooves of the Wild Hunt echoing through the night in times of danger reminds us—Cernunnos still guards His land and His people, the Witches."

Hawthorn

22nd Day	*This week is controlled by Luna and her dreams. Do not neglect your journal.*
23rd Day	*The solar or male energy bathes the fertile earth with the warmth of fire energy.*
24th Day	*Your solar energy will be expressed in the need to perfect your body and game skills.*
25th Day	*Your lunar energy will be expressed by the need to banish your friends and responsibilities. Collection, preparation and friends are equally important.*
26th Day	*Seeds planted at Beltane have taken root and are beginning to grow. Hawthorn begins and ends with cleansing, purification and conception.*
27th Day	*For centuries, Persephone appeared on this day at Lourdes, "Our Lady of Lourdes." Remember, you contain the seeds of the future.*
28th Day	*Thargelia, a purification ceremony for Diana as Artemis. Purify your life by removing all unhealthy habits, mental as well as physical. Lady Bless...*

The Totems of Hawthorn

Oak

There probably aren't too many people, attracted to this path, who haven't had an occasional, clear vision of the moonlight filtering through the gnarled branches of an Oak grove. This mystical sense of the Oak tree would almost seem to be a case of genetic memory, something in the blood. The fact is that generations of religious practitioners and mystics of western Europe gathered under the oaks to worship, to address the community, or prophesy. The tenacity and endurance of the mighty, abiding Oak was an emblem of survival and great age. These qualities assured the ancestors of the Celtic magical tradition that they had the right, the fittingness and the virtue to, like the Oak, survive the millenia.

It is difficult to kill an Oak tree. Fire, lightening, infestation, drought, or flood simply cause him to twist, bend, and adapt. Aside from outright clear-cut, there is little to shorten his life. Oak also establishes strong lineage. Acorns germinate and grow close to their parent, and are slow but tenacious in their maturation. To peoples living close to death, with the threat of total extinction ever at hand, this kind of survival ability was a powerful symbol.

Oak is another of the portal-type months. The strength of Oak is such that it is safe for you to go within, to the center of Self. The conscientious in-dwelling of the previous six months assure this. Oak stands at the boundary between the "dark" portion of the year and the "light" part of the year. He is called the "hinge" month, meaning that perspective can swing toward the past, as retrospection, or toward the future. The feeling is that, if you've made it this far, not much can threaten your journey from here on.

Fairy tales often feature a huge old Oak tree, with a door in its base. This door invariably opens onto other worlds and dimensions, and an adventure that takes the form of a Cosmic ascent or Underworld descent to the World Center (core of Self) where an initiatory trial awaits. Successfully conducted, this trial results in the Hera or Hero (candidate for initiation) inheriting great riches, or an invaluable prize (her or his own Self—Self possession and empowerment). The Celtic name for Oak is Duir, from the Gaelic Duir, derived from Indo-Aryan (Sanskrit) Duir. Duir means "door," and is the linguistic root of our modern word.

The "mighty oak" is well-known to most of us for its strength, endurance, and fine wood. It is often equated with quality and elegance. Historically, the Oak is associated with the Druids, the priestess and priest/hood of the Celtic people, and has been called the 'Druid's Door.' Oak groves were noteworthy as sacred places (as were groves of trees in general) and places of education. Druidic training, being an oral tradition, included the memorization and recitation of verse which 'contained' history and magic. The Oak is considered an oracular tree, one which provokes foreknowledge. The Bards, poet/ storytellers, undoubtedly memorized and spread some of these Druidic stories and through the natural process of evolution changed the stories by virtue of their own styles, thereby becoming caretakers of the archetypal development.

Dryads, or "tree spirits," may originally have been the priestesses, each of whom was entrusted with the care of a tree. Magically, anything which one tends becomes infused with one's "spirit," a phenomenon which is verified by practitioners of psychometry. In many parts of the ancient world, a "moon tree" was planted at the birth of a child, and their lives were considered linked.

The Oak's association with long memory reflects the Oak grove's place as an institution of learning or "university" (one place—all collected into one) of trees. The Oak groves' ability to retain knowledge and to house "tree spirits" emphasizes its durability. It also presages entry into other realms where the initiate may obtain knowledge and information from antiquity under guidance and protection.

The Oak's reputation as a tree of protection may spring from the fact that this tree is often the one in the forest that is likely to be struck by lightning and yet survive, thus sparing the other, less hardy trees. It is interesting to note that the expression "struck by lightning" is equated with the state of being inspired. Oak has also been used in the building of houses and ships, both protective containers for humans.

The rune for Oak is Dagaz, bringing breakthroughs, disintegration of old form, survival of the strongest into the new aeon, paradox, emergence of new generation, and doorways.

The Gaelic name for Oak is Duir, which reveals Sanskrit roots, and means door. The letter is D, and the Ogham symbol is shown below.

Rune
Dagaz

Ogham
Duir

Oak

April 18-24

1st Day	*As your lunar energy grows, think of yourself as a product. What does your label say? Ingredients? Directions?*
2nd Day	*In Bali, a women's celebration for the Goddess of Fruit. How will you honor Her?*
3rd Day	*Did you plant a tree or shrub? Did you eat a salad or paint a picture? All these are equally acceptable.*
4th Day	*Any action you take is a ritual when done with a clear intent. Drinking a glass of water to quench your thirst, or performing a rain dance to quench the parched earth are of equal importance.*
5th Day	*Sing to Ishtar for her hymns were stolen and sung to the male god who tried to supplant her.*
6th Day	*The Green Man or "Jack of the Woods," a forest god who impregnates barren women at Beltain. Children born of this mating are called Jackson, Robinson, or Woodsworth, etc.*
7th Day	*The green energy of spring impregnates us all if we are receptive and seeking. We must go, fearlessly, into the woods, for the reward is bountiful.*

The Oak Tree

The Priestess of Oak

The Celtic fire-holiday, Beltain, occurs during this lunar phase.

Jean—"One remnant of the Beltane celebration was still celebrated as late as the 1930's. Young people of both sexes created small baskets of Birch bark or Vine and filled them with moss and tiny bouquets of wildflowers. Before dawn on the first day of May (the central day of Oak month) the baskets were left on the doorsteps of friends and lovers. As the old English folk song said, "They were bringing summer in."

"Each flower had a very definite meaning. Compliments, good wishes and even proposals, in the language of flowers, were carried in "May baskets."

Each of us has our own symbols created by our life experiences. A rose will never be a symbol of love if it makes you sneeze. After suffering from a headache, you will forever remember a box of aspirin as a sign of loving care. This week create your own dictionary of symbols and their meanings for your personal use eg.:

Rose = _____   Feather = _____
Glamour = _____   Monday = _____
Sugar = _____   Pin = _____ etc.

The oak month will see your core strength emerge, as well as your native authority and perception. As this is a portal month, it opens a view into the past and the future. Visionary abilities are heightened as a result of your opened perception. Oak month stands at the intersection of the "dark" and "light" segments of the year, and as such is a gateway between the realms of Time.

Envision yourself in a grove of Oak trees. Feel the strength emanating from these great beings and let their grandness flow into you—affirming the life-giving force of the planet.

As you bask in the power that courses through you, let it caress and invigorate every cell of your body and every aspect of your mind and thoughts. Welcome the Lady as Druidess, knower of the secrets of Earth: peace, stability, productivity, growth! Allow Her to share this bounty with you. As you take Her hand, She shows you the doorway into the Center of the World—the center of yourself.

Look at this magnificent core; it glistens like a jewel set in a ring of precious metal. It is your essential Self—your strength, your authority. Herein lie the secrets of your very survival, your endurance and ability to adjust to the stresses in your life. Here is what carries you forward in the certain knowledge that you will survive—that you can accomodate change and keep going.

Experience the awe of this moment with the deity, and acknowledge the calm certainty of the Lady as She stands beside you. Know that you will retain the magic of this moment forever. As you release the Druidess' hand She points to a tree: is that your name you see shaped in the bark?

Oak, being the month of Beltane, is the time for fertility rites. What have you planted for yourself? How have you honored this new life, no less a child than an actual life of the flesh? What do you envision for this child of yours?

The Priestess of Oak is the Goddess expressing Herself as the Flower Maiden. She weds the Sun King, in a rite of mature and equal bonding. She brings to the fiery/active/masculine world of kinetic manifestation and creative expression the authority of Sovereignty, for she confers Balanced Power and the Right to Rule one's own Creative Will. She corresponds to the Empress card of the Major Arcana of the Tarot and is the flowering land, Herself.

Be aware of the flowers of creative manifestation around you, in your environment and in your consciousness. Honor your sovereign spirit with bowers of blossoming flowers and vines; indulge your senses and be aware of fragrances and pleasing textures. Beautiful music, paintings, films, plays, and wonderfully prepared food can be relished and treasured at this time. Esthetic appreciation of Divinity as perfection of function and form takes on the refined tone of a conscious ritual of respect for the creative/expressive spirit. This is a time to celebrate the World in the full-blown beauty of Her Power To Manifest.

To enjoy the World is an act of reverence—a worshipful stance which has the power to connect us to our own source of creativity.

Oak

8th Day	*As solar or male energy weakens salute the men in your life or the male energy in you, with gratitude, respect and love.*
9th Day	*A day began at noon when the sun was at its highest and continued until it returned again to the same place. Therefore, Beltain and Roodmass are one celebration, encompassing all aspects of light and darkness.*
10th Day	*St. Zita, Patron Saint of Housewives, is honored this day by male-dominated Christianity. The craft honors the Goddess in every aspect of her womanliness. Vesta, or Hestia, was the original (Occidental) Hearth Goddess.*
11th Day	*Floria — a day to ponder flower becoming fruit as reflected in a woman's life. Are you bud, flower, ripe fruit, or fruit dried to an incredible sweetness, containing the memory of sunshine, rain, sorrow and joy?*
12th Day	*Our ancestors needed a son to support, and a daughter to care for them in their old age. At the Beltane Feast, barren women were encouraged to mate with other men. These children were considered a gift from the gods and brought honor and joy to the family and community.*
13th Day	*Walpurgisnacht, Beltain or May Eve. Feast on all the special things you have been saving. A time to conceive the seed planted deep within you — maybe a career, profession, project, or relationship. Once planted, protect and nourish, this is your destiny.*
14th Day	*Roodmass. Gather flowers and foliage to surround the maypole, a symbol of male and female fertility. The red and white streamers? Blood and semen. Their action? Viewed from above, an inward and outward flowing spiral.*

The Priestess of Oak

The Hallows of Oak

With the Oak month, we come again into the realm of the Wand and the Pentacle. Oak wood has always had the talismanic properties of stability, peaceful productivity, and support. An authoritative survival virtuosity is bestowed by a wand or staff made of Oak wood. Holding an oaken staff or rod connects one with deep streams of survival logic, endurance and old knowledge. The oak wand is an aid to memory, and ancestral sophistication. An understanding of the ways in which our ancestors lived in harmony with the cycles of nature can be gained through working with the consciousness of Oak.

Of course, many other materials can be used in the making of powerful wands, some of them quite exotic:

Jessica—"My first wand came to my hand via a special friend with whom I worked one summer years ago. She was 'cleaning out her basement' with me when she found and and handed me a long, tapered 'stick,' and with a gleam in her eye she said to me, 'what do you think this is?'

"Without giving me much time to get my bearings, she went on to disclose the nature of the item, which was in fact an anatomical part of a bull, which had been stretched to about a yard in length. I will leave the details to your imagination. It is a fine implement, and has suited my purposes very well over the years. Needless to say, it is a tool which I reserve for very specific uses, it being a rather earthy device.

"My second wand followed fast upon the acquisition of the first one. It, too, came from a friend in a very matter-of-fact fashion. It is a lovely one, wooden, with a 'handle' shaped like the ball at the top of the legbone, which fits into the hip socket. I have had occasion to use this one as a walking stick when suffering from leg and foot injuries. It has always improved my state and, I feel, helped in the quick recoveries I have made. This wand is a friend, there when I've needed one.

"The third wand I acquired is straight out of every child's magic wand story. About a foot long, it is a tapered wooded one with a small, acorn-like tip. This one was an experimental piece produced by the son of one of my students while trying out his new power tools. It was love at first sight, but then I'm a true romantic at heart. This wand is very versatile, fitting nicely into a belt, is wonderful in the hand, and is made of Oak.

"Wands can be made of a variety of substances; I have a wand of about 7" in length, made of silver-sheen obsidian. This is a root-chakra wand to me, and used mainly for grounding, substantiating and securing rituals. I also have a beautiful suede-wrapped copper wand, decorated with feathers and tipped with a quartz crystal. It has been with me for about a year and a half, and so I consider it ready for use. It is very elegant and will like to be a participant in more public rituals.

"Perhaps one of the more unusual wands I was given came to me as a birthday gift. It is a Tibetan *vajra* (*dorje*—in Sanskrit) or 'thunderbolt,' a ritual implement representing the masculine principle. The *dorje* is always used in conjunction with the bell, which represents the feminine principle. I was not given a bell, but had always had one. Legend has it that the *dorje* 'falls from the sky or is found fully formed at the auspicious time.' Being a Tantrika, I have for many years had an interest in the Tibetan Buddhist philosophy. The 'thunderbolt' is a sacred symbol for me as I was give the name of the Germanic thunder god (Tina) at birth."

Oak

15th Day	*This sensible and independent action to preserve families upon the festival of Beltane was seen as licentious and orgiastic and downright pleasurable by the enraged male clergy and led to the persecution of the witches.*
16th Day	*Bono Dea — a women's festival for public welfare. In a circle of women, build a fire, place beside it a container of water, and bless the four corners and directions. Jump over the embers or toss round objects, fruit, coins, cheese, while making a wish. Water over the fire ends the rite.*
17th Day	*Sheela Na Gig, her open and exposed genitalia, represents the door of life. We hung old clothes on the Hawthorn tree to honor her. Give clothes to a women's transition house. Sacrifice one thing you love.*
18th Day	*Boy's Day in Japan—mothers honor their sons and the magic they possess. If you don't have a son, borrow one. Little boys smell of grass, fresh air, and roses. (Old ones don't.)*
19th Day	*Today Hathor visits Nut, Mother of the Goddesses and Gods. Visit the mother of your personal, living Goddesses.*
20th Day	*It is time to name your personal Goddesses. We submit Jessica/Isis, Tara/Bast, Yvonne/Neb-Thet, Jean/Seline.*
21st Day	*Furry dance to honor Maid Marian as the female part of the Green Man. Feel your bare feet on the grass.*

The Hallows of Oak

The Totems of Oak

The Venus-ruled sign of Taurus conforms to this month. The Bull, like the Oak, is an earthy consort-lover of the moon. This was ever his role in the Venus ruled matriarchies of the Age of Taurus (7,500—5,000 BCE, roughly).

The Sacred Cow of India is Kali, the Mother Goddess, and the Cow-eared Goddess, Hathor, was the predecessor of Isis in the archaic Egyptian divine hierarchy. Osiris' spiritually evolved aspect was the Apis, or Moon-Bull. The Hebrews reverted to their roots when they angered Moses by making a "Golden Calf" for their mobile temple in the Sinai desert. Irish Queen Maeb stopped at nothing to procure for herself a certain "Brown Bull" from a neighboring king, and our fairytales and nursery rhymes contain references to our historic Celtic bovine cult with "The cow jumped over the Moon." The Irish Cow Goddess was called "Boann," and is possibly the oldest of the Indo-European (Aryan) Goddesses of that land. Druidic ceremonies for May Day featured large herds of oxen in procession with an "Ark" carried by celebrants from a Holy Isle in a river or lake. It was an old custom (and still is in parts of India) to garland a cow or a bull for May Day, or other holidays. The cow was considered a symbol of the land itself, in this context, producing nurture and flowers in abundance. The Milky Way is an expression of Nut, originally a form of Hathor, the Cow Mother of Egypt. The Celtic feeling that cattle equated to stability and wealth probably travelled into Western Europe with the Indo-Aryans, whose *Rg Veda* (Aryan religious scripture) invokes all things good: "Lions, Chariots, and many fine Cattle."

The bull has long been associated with the moon, evidence of which remains in the stories of ancient Crete where the moon goddess was named Tauropolos. The Summerian moon-god was called "Sin," and "Min" (which meant "moon") and this name later turned up in that of Minoas, King Minos of Minoan Crete, and that of the creature that gave him a bad name, the Minotaur (which means "Moon-Bull"). The Minotaur was actually the fabrication of the fear of Solar-oriented Achaean Greeks and Mycenaeans who, encountering the cultus of the Moon-Bull (lunar sexuality) and depictions of the bull-dance, thought that these signs indicated a malefic lunar monstrosity that devoured virgins and to whom sacrifices must be made. The bull-dance, shown on many urns and vases of Minoan Crete, was an initiatory exercise for adolescent athletes of both sexes. The bull-dance signified victory over one's own fearful animal nature. Achaean Greek mythologizing cast the Minotaur as the offspring of the moon Goddess, Pasiphae, and a white bull. The white bull was also central in the cult of Mithras, the bull-slayer. Bull slaying may have originated with the choosing of a surrogate for the king who would be ritually executed at the end of his reign to insure the future fertility of the land, a concept illustrated in the myths of Ishtar and Tammuz and Venus and Adonis, where the Goddess loses her consort to the Queen or Goddess of the Underworld (her own devourer aspect).

The bull-slaying ceremony persists to this day in the bullfight of Spain, considered astrologically to be a Scorpio country. Scorpio is the opposite sign to Taurus and rules the month diametrically opposed to Oak month on the Wheel, Birch. Samhain (All Hallows) begins Birch month, and the "dark" half of the year. Beltane (May Eve) begins Oak month, and the "light" half of the year. In a well-known Roman sculpture of Mithras (or Vedic "Mitra") slaying the Bull, close examination will reveal a scorpion clasping the genitals of the Bull in its pincers. Scorpio rules the genitals. The sting of certain varieties of scorpions is deadly and this insect is not above turning the deadly sting upon itself, given enough provocation. The bullfight retains overtones of the desire to overcome the animalistic and instinctual tendencies inherent in human nature.

Oak

May 9-15

22nd Day	*Lemuria—brings gifts to the ashes of the dead. Make gestures of peace with the dead even if they are only dreams or promises.*
23rd Day	*Tin Hau, Goddess of the North Star, helps us find out where we are.*
24th Day	*We live in a dream of projection. Put signs around your environment saying, "Stop what you are doing and describe it: I am turning a cold water tap, I am opening a drawer." Be here now. Do not anticipate or recall.*
25th Day	*Sashti is a pan-like forest God. Revel in the scent of moss, leaf-mold and musk. Real or imaginary living God? Either can be pleasurable or fulfilling. Happy Birthday, Florence Nightingale.*
26th Day	*Neptune's turn, toss flowers into running water in his name.*
27th Day	*Black-clad Isis Tithe: If you have prospered this year, in Isis' name give money to her special causes, or buy books for yourself in her honor.*
28th Day	*In Rome, Vesta. In Greece, Maia. And in Guatemala, Rain Dances. All honor water as our beginning and our rebirth. Drum softly, like raindrops awakening the earth to new life.*

The Totems of Oak

Holly

The Holly month is a warrior moon. Holly energy is scrappy, feisty and won't be cowed by anything. It is a time when natural, life-affirming combativeness is aroused. A natural, personal and tribal dignity is present, and is scornful of attempts to squash or oppress it.

The Holly is a tree that displays a defiant life-energy, even in the face of winter. When the rest of the world succumbs to a sedative layer of snow, and all systems have slowed beneath the contracting cold, Holly's vital sap continues to invigorate the brilliantly green, spiny leaves and blood-red berries. Holly is symbolic of the life energy being conserved within like a potent, inner light.

This vitality, associated with virility, was regarded as sacred by ancient peoples, and the name, "Holly," means "holy." The belief is preserved in Christian folk-ways; Holly is traditional decor for Christmas, and Celtic tree lore was preserved in the Christmas carol, "The Holly and The Ivy."

The wood of the Holly tree is uniformly dense, and evenly weighted. It was used for spear and chariot shafts, the magic of battle-readiness thereby ingrained into the warriors' tools of war. The Holly tree is a champion and protector, its wood-formed palisades and battlements to ward off attackers and marauders. The feeling of Holly is loyalty to dependents and protection of those who are vulnerable or victimized. The vindication of rights and clarification of claims and grievances are activities of this lucid month.

Lleu, Lew, Lu, and Lugh are ancient names for the hero as spearman and protector. As Llew Llaw Gyffes, he was known as "The Spearman With the Long Shaft," "The Long-armed Spearman," or "He of the Quick Hand," an image that evokes the long, penetrating rays of the sun, or bolts of lightning. This name expressed the phallic light-god whose mandate was justice for the oppressed or persecuted. Lancelot and Lohengren inherited the traits of these archaic, Celtic god-forms. Lucina is their Goddess/heroine counterpart. Lucifer, whose name (before it was demonized by the dualism of Zoroastrianism and Judeo-Christianity) meant "Lightbearer," also shares the lineage of the root word "Lu," which means "Light," hence "lucid," "luminous," "illumination," "translucence," etc. Lucifer and the other banished angels were said to have fallen from heaven as snakes with gem-stones in their foreheads—an image evocative of lightening zig-zagging to earth.

Lancelot was trained at arms by The Lady of the Lake, and sent forth into the world to serve Sovereignty as Champion. He marries the Lady of the Grail Castle, Elaine, and retires to a castle in the middle of a lake called "Joyous Garde." Lohengren had a similar apprenticeship in a sacred mountain within the precinct of a "Grail Castle."

Traditionally a wood used in the fashioning of spears, Holly is associated with the Warrior. His Gaelic name, Tinne, is reminiscent of the German thundergod—Tina, the pronunciation being the same. The literal translation of Tinne is "Sacred Tree" and so we see that Holly was held in very high regard by the ancients. Holly was also held sacred to the Germanic Holle, or Hel, the underworld Goddess who presided over death and regeneration.

The Druids considered Holly the winter abode of the wood spirits (or dryads) and so considered him to be a protection against ill fortune. Christianity embraced Holly as a symbol of "sacrifice," and saw the Christ's crown of thorns as being of Holly leaves—the bright red berries being representative of the blood of the Passion shed on the Cross. The red berries are also associated with the color of life as well as menstrual blood.

According to tradition, Holly planted near a house would offer protection against lightning and witchcraft but, as we have seen, Holly is sacred to the Lords of thunder and lightning. As has been mentioned previously, the best way (where persecution exists) to ensure the presence of an important plant is to say its purposes and uses are opposite to what they are in actuality. German witches were (and possibly still are) known to make wands out of the wood of the Holly tree.

Medicinally the leaves of the Holly have been used by herbalists to relieve coughs, colds, flu, fevers and rheumatism. The berries are quite toxic and have a severe purging effect.

The Rune for the Holly month is Tiwaz, invoking direct action, the spear, the warrior/shaman, negotiation, and the surrender of self for the common benefit.

The Gaelic name for Holly is Tinne, the letter is T, and the Ogham symbol is shown below.

Rune
Tiwaz

Ogham
Tinne

Holly

May 16-22

1st Day	*We begin a month of challenge. Here we encourage you to fight for our beliefs and to keep safe the precious gift we carry within.*
2nd Day	*The Celtic time of ripening—hard green sour berries become rich, ripe, sweet nourishment and pleasure. Seek the ripe sweetness within you.*
3rd Day	*Feast in honor and gratitude to the horned god and celebrate his freedom.*
4th Day	*Today he is replaced by Bendis, Goddess of the Hunt. Feel her power; it is yours.*
5th Day	*Debra Sampson joined the Continental Army on this day in 1762. Sometimes it is necessary for women to become warriors. Is now your time?*
6th Day	*Kallyntria Plynteria—clean and nurture the sacred places in yourself and in your life.*
7th Day	*Cascia of Spain bids you be merciful to your past. Forgive yourself.*

The Holly Tree

The Priestess of Holly

The night is dark and clear. Although the temperature is quite warm, you shiver as though suddenly gripped by icy fingers. Your senses are alert, sharp! You sniff the air like an animal anticipating danger.

With your night vision, you notice a form in the darkness in front of you. Instinct tells you to run but something else entices you to stay and investigate this stranger. Stock-still, you watch in silence. The figure remains as still as you are. In the darkness you make out the form of someone holding what seems to be a spear. Just as recognition dawns, the figure poises as if to throw the spear in your direction. Startled, you cry out and the action is checked—though the spear remains poised.

"Who are you?" The words fly from you, almost against your will.

"Who are you?" comes the reply.

This is the Goddess, Holle, guardian of underworld realms and keeper of the knowledge of the hidden places. The Shamanic Path always demands an encounter with the Goddess of Death and Regeneration in one or many of Her guises. It is here you come face to face with your deadly fears, your dark twin, your Shadow Self.

As you face your Goddess self, recognize and acknowledge your fears, your supposed weaknesses, and your ability to survive and transform experience. Take this power with you into your everyday life.

The warrior "Light God," Lugh or Llew Llaw Gyffes, has a female counterpart. Her name is Lucina, and versions of Her are to be found in the mythology of cultures ranging from east of the Black Sea, to North Africa, to France and Scandinavia. She is related to the "Eye Goddesses" of the Middle East through Her kinship with Lilith and Mari. The "Fairy Melusina" is an aspect of Lucina, and was worshipped at Lusinia—modern day Lusignon. Lucina is the original version of the "St. Lucies" of Christian orthodoxy. "St. Lucy" is reverenced by a festival of lights, candles or lanterns, and is the patron saint of eyesight. Her martyrdom propaganda depicts her with her eyes on a platter, as if offering them to heaven. The pseudo-history of her plight is that she put out her own eyes rather than witness her forced marriage to a pagan lord. This is a patently false fabrication regarding the archetype who bears the name "Lucy." Her original form was a great Goddess, patroness of Clarity of Vision, Justice, and Insight. Her megalithic statues had brilliant, facetted sapphires as the eyes, and were vandalized by pious Christians early in the millenium. Hence the myth accounting for the loss of her eyes. Lucina stood for the Inner Light (or Soul) that is visible as a kind of brilliance, gleam or spark of consciousness, in the eyes.

The story of Melusina bears a resemblance to that of Lilith of Mesopotamia. Melusina was the "maiden of the well," who dwelt in the grotto where the river's source issued from the rock. She gave food and drink to weary travellers, and gave healing to all those who were ailing in body or spirit. One day the Duke Raymond came to the well. He was wounded from a battle and sick at heart. He heard a beautiful voice singing, and then he saw the maiden, bathed in light. She was sitting on a stone in the middle of the pool, singing and playing a harp, her long, serpent's tail swishing in the water. When she saw the wounded warrior, she stopped singing. She grew legs and stepped upon the shore and came to him, bringing him nurture and healing in her silver chalice filled with the holy water of her realm.

The Duke was healed of his wounds and heart's sorrow, and asked the fairy maiden to marry him. Melusina said that she would—on one condition, that being that he never invade the privacy of her bath of the Sabbath Eve, for then she must leave him. Duke Raymond agreed to this, and so Melusina accompanied him to his castle and they were wed. They lived happily for many years, their only sorrow being that their sons were somehow monstrous—having three eyes, large fangs, or being of supernatural size. Other than this life went smoothly, and Melusina became renowned for her civilizing arts. She was called the "Builder of Cities," for all the castles, walled cities, towns, roads, and strongholds that she built. The wealth and fame of her family increased, and all was going well—but then Duke Raymond became curious. He wondered why he must not gaze upon his wife in her bath of the Sabbath Eve, and he resolved to peer through the keyhole to find out.

What he saw through the keyhole amazed him, for there was Melusina in her giant, gilded bath, combing her long, golden hair and singing—with a scaly, serpent's tail lashing the water into a swirling froth. The moment Raymond saw her, Melusina ceased her singing. She grew webby wings like a dragon, and issued a mournful keening. She flew from her bath and entered the wind that moaned and howled around the highest tower of the castle. And there she remained—returning only to give her mournful cry whenever one of her descendants passed over into death.

Melusina's serpent tail and webbed wings are also features of the Lamia, and of Lilith. The shrieking, as of wind, is a trait of Lilith—and also the monstrous children. The esoteric "Sabbath Eve" is Friday—or Freya day, the Sabbath being Yahweh's day—or Saturn day. Friday is ruled by and named for Venus/Freya—who is fish or serpent-tailed, and who comes on the Sabbath Eve as the Shekina, or "bride."

Holly

May 23-29

8th Day	*Rosalia. Before Christianity, women made sweet-smelling beads of rose petals, allowing them to dry in the Holly breeze, strung in series of five to signify fire, water, earth and air—crowned by spirit, the pentacle of witches.*
9th Day	*A gypsy day to tell fortunes and dance and sing about really important issues—life, death and beauty that you create.*
10th Day	*Tao, The Way—Mother of the World Path of the Heart. Meditate on truth in nature. Do not destroy or interfere, but flow like the river.*
11th Day	*Rhoda had her breast removed. Five days later she was on a walking tour of Israel. Her credo—the Amazons removed their breast so that their arrows flew straight.*
12th Day	*Chin Haw Fu Jen celebrates the Amazon Goddess. Ninety pounds and five feet tall, Rhoda is my Amazon and my hero for a million other reasons. Feel her strength and use it in your life.*
13th Day	*During Pythia the sacred snakes licked Cassandra's ears and gave her the secret gift of true prophecy. You have the same gift for the sacred snakes are your sexuality.*
14th Day	*Ambarvalia. Clean your hearth and wherever fires dwell in your house, in the name of the lares, household fire gods.*

The Priestess of Holly

The Hallows of Holly

A staff, or great-wand, that acts as a stave or spear (or lightning shaft) is the image of the magical tool suggested by the energy of Holly month. You've met the hero who goes by the names of Llew, Lugh, Llew Llaw Gyffes or Lancelot and who is known as "the Long-Armed Spearman." And you have already met Holle, the Warrioress of the Underworld, in the visualization of the Priestess of Holly. These archetypes are light deities who live, work, and fight in the medium of the "Dark," and exemplify the fighting, or reforming, Will. They are at home in this medium, and their job is to illuminate the content and power of the subconscious realms—the "Otherworld" that underwrites and gives rise to the visible, or created, world.

Any talisman that accompanies your ventures into the mystical and potent causal realm of your own, creative levels is the perfect instrument with which to orchestrate the energies of Holly, but respond to your own promptings to act in accordance with this month. The Mercurial rulership of Gemini activates the Will, so the Magician's card from the Tarot is appropriate here, as well as the Lovers' card. The Magician acts, in Accordance with the Will, and chooses from the tools of every element upon his altar. Therefore, any instrument is appropriate to Holly month, as a matter of conscious choice.

Yvonne—"Once, when I was living and working in Alaska for about half a year, a friend of mine was worried about some forays I was making into the realms of sex and new relationship. She worried about me for an entire week, while I was off with a new lover that she didn't know or trust. I had left in a cloud of rebellion toward her disapproval of this man. On a black motorcycle, he and I headed North into the Yukon.

"My friend wept and worried, called the police on both sides of the border, and sat down to carve me a wand. The wand emerged from the wood to be long, tapered and elegant. It was tipped with a pair of wings near the tip, or operative end. An airy quartz crystal was bound into the tip, like a nose-cone. I called the wand "Dragon Queen," for its fiery quality of flight.

"Dragon Queen is a warriors' tool. She is vigilant, protective, and fearless. She provides her own light upon a matter, and she travels well. In fact, for a time, I couldn't manage to keep her out of cars that were bound for other lands. She's cruised from the Yukon through Southeast Alaska, to British Columbia and Washington state without me, because I couldn't manage to keep her out of travellers' cars. She's settled down these days, and limits her flights to the realm of dream travel."

Jean— "If you stand up straight with your feet apart, spread your arms wide enough to embrace the whole world, and hold your head high, you will be a perfect five pointed star—Spirit, Earth, Water, Fire, and Air—the elements that make up the Universe. The top point is Spirit, the one thing that sets each of us apart from all else.

"I had always loved the silver stars worn by our Elders, the sacred symbol of the Goddess. During my studies several pentacles came to me. Some stayed with me; others were quickly passed on to others who admired or needed them. Once I had an ancient silver coin melted down and made into a pentacle, believing erroneously that money was the strongest force on Earth. Older and wiser, I was touched when a young woman brought me her newly made pentacle. It was absolutely perfect—each point exact. Each line crossed at the right spot and every angle was correct. It was beautiful and delicate as a spider web. The young woman said, "I spent hours; I swore and cursed it. I worked and reworked it. My hands were bruised and bleeding, but I finished it and it is right and perfect. I put so much anger into it—I feel you are the only person on Earth strong enough to control it. Please accept it with my love and respect."

"I had known her for years—a young woman with many rough edges, quick to anger and often at sword's point with the other students. That night the Goddess blessed her for her devotion and her perseverance. As she walked away her face was smooth and serene. She moved with grace and dignity, all anger and tension left behind in the pentacle. With grace and confidence she served for many years as a High Priestess and won the respect of all who worshipped with her. I still treasure her pentacle and wear it frequently.

"Although I had always resented restrictions, I reached a time in my life when I was forced to follow a strict dietary routine. The most irritating part was that each morning at ten, and each afternoon at two, I had to eat a half a piece of fruit. It seemed to me that half a bananna or peach was wasteful and stupid, and each day I became more resentful. All of my negative emotions were focussed on a silly piece of fruit.

"My daughter and I travel often; the long trips by car and ferry give us special time. We leave before dawn and, in those dark hours devoted to Hecate, we are able to discuss and solve all of life's complicated issues. Secure in our car, each morning at ten, I take a red apple from my bag and polish until it glows. With my Blade, I cut it—not from stem to blossom-end—but across its circumference, exposing the five-pointed star at its heart—the sacred pentacle of the Goddess.

"Tara and I share the bounty of the Goddess. Her pentacle protects our travels and her fruit replenishes our bodies. The pentacle comes in many forms and in many materials. Open your eyes and you will find it everywhere."

Holly

May 30-June 5

15th Day	*Leap upon your broom and run around a newly planted field, leaping into the air to show the crop how high to grow. An explanation for a belief that witches could fly? Think again.*
16th Day	*Joan of Arc was burned at the stake on this day. Her crime? She was strong, honest, did everything that was expected of her, and did it successfully.*
17th Day	*Today Carna gives access to suppressed information: "You can be more than you dream." Find the truth you need.*
18th Day	*Cardea, a day to honor women in public life. Write a letter, make a call. Say "Good job."*
19th Day	*Cassandra's gift? Prophecy. Her curse? No one ever believed her. Did you find that out for yourself? Did you think it was just you? Did you let it stop you? Be valiant.*
20th Day	*A day for old maids and free women, two extinct species. They were the only women with rights of self-determination—the subject of cruel jokes, but other women were chattel and wards.*
21st Day	*Pioneers in all the arts, educators of children and care-givers, underpaid and discriminated against with contempt. We honor you as heroic, as warriors.*

The Hallows of Holly

The Totem of Holly

Swans were considered a royal animal in ancient Britain and were often provided with nesting areas in the moats of large castles. This also underscored their fabled defensiveness, for there is nothing so ferocious as an aroused swan. They will extend their long necks and fly directly at an intrusive presence or marauder. Besides their fearless defense of nesting areas or territory, they are gracefully beautiful birds, expressing a harmony of movement and form that is easy to construe as "royal." They swim in pairs and defend their mates zealously. They seem proud of their familial bonds.

Across Siberia, Russia, Northern Greece, Turkey, and Eastern Europe a recurring sculptural design has been found by the efforts of archeology. It is a figure—stylized and graceful, minimilistic and sophisticated in its simplicity. It is the shape of a guitar body, violin, or cello. This figure, its incidence spanning thousands of miles (Siberia, Russia, Anatolia, Old Europe), and thousands of years in its manufacture (c. 8,000 BCE—5,000 BCE), has been catalogued by Russian art historians as "figures of birds."

This is an oversimplification, for they are not merely "figures of birds" but also bodies of women (many are detailed with breasts and vulvae) while they are also phallic, with penile heads, and embody the impetus of flight and music. They are the ubiquitous, androgynous figure of the Age of Gemini (roughly 8,000 BCE—5,000 BCE), and they combine the phallic thrust of an aroused will with the shape-giving power of the womb—the neck and body of a stringed instrument. On a mundane level, they most nearly resemble the posture of a swan with wings held out to dry and neck fully extended.

Jessica—"Holly month is synonymous with the zodiacal Gemini, popularly the Twins. There are many myths of these Gemini twins, the earliest representing them not as same sex siblings but as heterosexual lovers (hence the Lovers' Tarot card rulership of Gemini). I have come to regard Gemini as the sign of intimacy, total sharing of oneself with another. This element of intimacy (into-me-see) is reflected in the modern myths of the Greek and Roman cultures: Castor and Polydeuces are two brothers, one of which is a (mortal) artist and the other being an (immortal) warrior. Their love for each other is unsurpassed and when Polydeuces is mortally wounded, his brother, Castor, intervenes on his behalf in order that the two of them not be permanently parted. Zeus granted Castor's request and allowed that both twins would spend half the year in the Underworld and the other half of the year on Mount Olympus, giving rise to the concept of the light and dark aspects of character for which Gemini is noted.

"The Twins are also patrons of athletes and athletic arts, as well as guardians of sailors—implying an intimate connection to that other "sacred tree," the Ash—associated with Poseidon.

"In some Pagan/Wiccan traditions, midsummer represents a time of turning of the moon from waxing to waning. The Oak King reigns during the waxing part of the year to midsummer at which point is then defeated by the Holly King and so withdraws his influence during the waning part of the year. Once again the theme of light and dark is presented.

"Duality, for me, is best expressed in the concept of the lovers: favoring the Jungian idea of the inherent masculine (animus) in women and feminine (anima) in men, I see Holly/Gemini as representing our continued striving towards wholeness, the integration of the duality of our own natures, the blending of the light and dark aspects of ourselves. The warrior Holly becomes for me the spiritual warrior under whose protection we sacrifice ("make sacred") ourselves in the interest of human evolution as well as the evolution of consciousness.

"Being a native of the astrological sign Gemini, I have come to truly appreciate the mystical implications of Holly, the "sacred tree." At birth I was named 'Tina' (the same as the Germanic warrior god) by my parents, which aptly describes my basic nature, though I have chosen to be known by the name I received upon taking my first vows. I credit my German ancestral memories for my interest in the Runes and I use a lovely handmade set of Holly Runes for readings."

The version of Leda's involvement with the Swan that has been most promulgated in this recent, patriarchal age is that of her rape by the Swan, as a disguise for a criminally motivated Zeus. But the real association of Leda and the Swan is the fact that Leda is the Swan, in one of her shape-shifting manifestations. The Swan is Leda's totem, not her rapist. Leda is also known as Lat, Latona, Al Lat (later masculinized as Allah) who, in her Swan or Goose form, conceived and hatched the World Egg. From the Egg, Castor and Pollux (Polledeucis) were born, although in their original form in the style of the Age of Gemini (approximately 8000 BCE—5500 BCE) they were male and female twins. Their polarity remained a non-combative, mutually creating dynamic throughout the Age of Taurus (approximately 5500 BCE—3000 BCE), but became the battleground of Dualism in the Age of Aries (approximately 3000 BCE—500 BCE) showing the influence of ideologies such as Zoroastrianism and the Vedas. The gradual polarization of opposites hostile to each other grew from the original concept of the Swan (Leda)'s World Egg which contained and incubated all possibilities.

Holly

22nd Day	*Examine your braid. Do you need to add new relationships? Does your cobweb need new and different goals? How have you changed? Are you ready to slay a dragon or bake a cake? We admire and honor you for either achievement.*
23rd Day	*Vestalia. Truth is a thunderbolt that ignites the flames of change. Examine the lies you tell yourself.*
24th Day	*Grain in the Ear Festival of China. (Do not stuff rice in your ear.) See how full the seed you planted at Beltain is becoming. Time to nourish and share it with a few special friends.*
25th Day	*Mater Matuta—Become mother to yourself. Support, nourish, and comfort you. Then teach yourself something new.*
26th Day	*Be a mother to those who are not your children. Remember the woman in your childhood who did this for you—even if it only happened for a moment, it happened and it made a difference.*
27th Day	*Did you comfort, nourish, nurse, support, or rebuke? Why?*
28th Day	*Write a personal story about you as a hero, amazon, or warrior.*

The Totem of Holly

Hazel

The Salmon of Wisdom became so because he swallowed nine of the enchanted Hazel nuts as they fell into the stream in which the Salmon swam. Nine is the number of the Muses, the Clan Mothers of the Paleolithic, the Priestesses of the Sacred Isle of Women of Celtic Tradition, and the Goddess number of "completion" and finality. The Hazel nuts gave Salmon the comprehensive wisdom that is their magical property.

The Hazel is a tree with an uncommon affinity for water, and as such obtains insight and inspiration. Hazel branches are the wood commonly used for water-divination. Magically, Hazel can be used to divine essential value, content, and meaning. Hazel wands cut straight to the source and penetrate the inner truth of issues and events.

Hazel is the natural ally of diviners of all types. The tremulous vibration of ley lines and vortices can be gauged and measured with this delicate instrument. The "truth" of fairness, proportion and balance is rendered by Hazel's insightful measure. The vibratory sentience of the wood is so acute that it is electrical in nature, and acts something like a receiver for creative inspiration. Hazel is awakening and enlivening to the senses. It is conductive and magnetic, creating a flow of intuitive energy. It is like quicksilver in its communication of intuition to ideas and realization. Hazel is a "wise" tree, and serves as a tool of the diplomat or adjudicator. The pliancy of Hazel makes it well-suited to this task.

Hazel nuts were once thought to contain enlightenment, visions, and poetic inspiration. This month falls under the influence of Cancer, the watery denizen of deep emotions and sensitive perception. This is a month when deeply submerged wisdom may emerge into conscious awareness. The encoded, genetic wisdom of generations of female ancestors may come forward to inspire the actions of the present, for this is the time of Mother-Wisdom. The Isis-like ability to intuitively know what is right in certain situations may inform your choices, and if you choose to verbalize your choices, your words will be well-chosen and judicious. You may find that you have the capacity to inspire others, and they you. Flow of energy is the character of this month, and an appreciation for the fertile and renewing properties of water.

Hazel bespeaks ties and linkages. Being associated with the zodiacal sign of Cancer, which is itself indicative of family connections and history, Hazel has been used as a means to find one's way to the source. Hazel branches have natural source-finding abilities.

In order to not repeat the past, one must be in touch with it. This is the domain of Hazel as holder of historical records. Hazel is also associated with leylines and straight tracks, power centers and their connectors. In keeping with the tradition of Hazel, this makes for a very interesting research project into the past, our planetary history.

Hazel also concerns herself with boundaries, both psychic and manifest. She is a tree of mediation, which helps one to discern personal space as well as one's way in the outer world. Her gift is divination, a word which by its very sound recalls to us our connection to the Divine within ourselves, our own personal Great Mother. Her ability to enable us to create linkages helps us form a bridge between the conscious and unconscious self, allowing us immediate access to our intuitive and ancestral knowledge/wisdom, an expression of psychic mediation, or soul contact.

Nut trees of all types are characteristic of this month, and of the hard-shelled richness of its Cancerian quality. The Apple tree shares this month, called "Quert" in the Ogham tree calendar, and fruit trees of all kinds are appropriate to remember here.

Jean—"Walnut trees in Saxon and Celtic lore were linked to the classical triple lunar Goddess. The tree branches and roots symbolized the nymph or maiden, the flowers symbolized the beauty of a totally fulfilled woman, and the nut or fruit—the wisdom of the crone. The complete nourishment (15% protein and 60% fat) in a handy, hermetically sealed container made it the royal or noble tree of the Romans. The Walnut kernel, because of its resemblance to the brain, was used as sympathetic magic to treat mental illness and brain fevers. This early association with insanity is ironic in view of the modern derisive term that describes an insane person as being "nuts." In the seventeenth century young men were required to plant a certain number of Walnut trees before they were allowed to wed. Walnuts were a magical tool used in marriage rituals—walnuts picked from the ground were spread lavishly on the floor and under the bed during the wedding festivities. Each crushed or broken Walnut signified a healthy child. A woman hoping to delay childbearing would hide a walnut in the bodice of her wedding gown—one for each year that she wished to remain childless. Needlework or jewelry in the shape of a Walnut was equally effective."

Hazel month spans the Summer Solstice and the event of the sun entering the sign of Cancer. At the solstice, called Alban Heruin by the Druids, the sun reaches its zenith in the Northern Hemisphere, providing the greatest number of hours of sunlight of the year. From this point the light will decrease daily to its nadir—the shortest day of the year or Winter Solstice.

The Hazel Rune is Kaunaz, meaning hearthfire, forge, creativity, passion, craft, and instinctiveness.

The Gaelic name for Hazel is Coll, the letter is C, and the Ogham symbol is shown below.

Rune
Kaunaz

Ogham
Coll

Hazel

June 13-19

1st Day	*Epona, the Horse Goddess, blesses women's independence and their dreams of freedom. Controlling a horse proved you could control your life. A car is a poor substitute but it works for me. Name your transportation (magic carpet).*
2nd Day	*Light a birthday candle for the muse who inspires you. With her sisters, she stands at your left shoulder, whispering her wisdom in your ear. Listen...*
3rd Day	*Calliope brings epic song, Clio—history, Euterpe—lyric songs, Thalia—comedy, Melpomene—tragedy, Terpsichore—dance, Erato—erotic poetry, Polyhymnia—sacred hymns, Urania—astronomy.*
4th Day	*Not inspired? Then try Mnemosyne, the mother of all muses. Her gift is memory.*
5th Day	*Day of Eurydice, prisoner of the Underworld, whose name we remember. In 1963, the first woman in space—her name forgotten, listed only as woman.*
6th Day	*Eurydice was a beauty and her story one of love. The space woman was a Russian worker. Is it only love and beauty that is remembered? Who failed to give her name? The "Whole Woman Calendar."*
7th Day	*List the nameless women who have given you love, care, kindness and support. Telephone operators, nurses, waitresses and on and on...*

The Hazel Tree

The Priestess of Hazel

You emerged from the waters of your mother's womb, the great oceanic depths of a woman who came from her mother and she from her mother before her. This line is unbroken throughout all His/Herstory, whether or not it is recorded in written words. You are the living proof as is everyone else on this planet.

The story of your ancestors is encoded in your DNA and in the deep memories which form part of our collective unconsciousness; they are timeless, flowing forward into your future and backwards into your past.

Sit in quiet meditation and welcome dialogue respectfully with one of your own ancestors. Repeat this exercise often and develop a conscious friendship with this predecessor. Allow her/him to tell you of the experiences which inform you now so that you may appreciate another aspect of the human story.

As you become friends with this ancestor, construct an altar in her/his honor. Allow your ancestor to become an Ally; permit your Ally to guide you in the assembly of the altar. Participate wholeheartedly in the experience. Remember, you are also honoring yourself.

When you feel you have completed the process with this ancestor, begin again with another following the same sequence. You may continue to add to the already existing altar until it becomes a collective altar.

Another exercise is to stand in the pentacle (star) formation. Be aware of your own mother standing behind you and her mother behind her and her mother behind her in a continuum to the infinite horizon. Feel the powerful woman connection flowing through all of you and forward into the children of your own body or mind.

Many traditions practice ancestor worship, honoring those who have gone before and who have left their legacy. Linking to ancestral wisdom and informing it with our current knowledge will enable us to proceed more wisely into our collective future. Hazel connotes "female wisdom," and is considered a Witch tree ("Witch Hazel"). The Celtic Sea God, Mannanan, is associated with Hazel. Mannanan had a "Crane Bag," which contained all the esoteric wisdom of the Druids, including poetry, chants, incantations, divination, symbolism, history, and the lore and secret significance of all things. That this knowledge was considered "Woman's Magic" from the earliest times is evident in the legend that the Crane Bag was made from the skin of a woman. (Magic women were thought to be capable of shape-shifting into Crane form.) In other words, woman contained the wisdom, like the Hazel nuts.

Every woman carries within her the genetic code that marked the evolution of the First Woman. The "Mitochondrial Eve" theory refers to this phenomenon, whereby each woman carries the DNA or genetic blueprint of the first human female in the mitocondria, or lining, of every cell. The evolutionary changes that render us "human" are passed on through the female line. This is why sovereignty and "royal blood" was originally only traced through the mother, and why "kingship" was conferred through marriage to the Queen. The antiquity of this practice is evident by the fact that Pharaoh obtained the throne of Egypt (itself considered to be Isis) by marriage to a daughter of the royal line, which lies behind the incidence of incestuous marriage within the royal house. This belief was an accurate assessment that the royal blood of Isis, the divine ancestress, was passed from mother to daughter. Isis, Herself, is a concept of genetic memory, wisdom, and maternal protection and resurrection. As the Divine Ancestress, She is the human Clan Mother, and the actual stuff of her original design passes, intact, through the female line. An understanding of this underscored the most ancient concepts of the Goddess held by our ancestors.

Hazel

8th Day	*Ix Chel, a Mayan Goddess of Stars and Children, another aspect of Jessica, astrologer and mother.*
9th Day	*Longest day, shortest night, a day for the bitter sweetness of honey, for the winter is coming. Goddess chant: "In summer's heat, her kisses are sweet, for she sings in leafy bowers..."*
10th Day	*We call it a spell because it should be carefully considered and spelled out. If we called it a blessing, would people fear us less?*
11th Day	*On midsummer night Cerridwen stirs her cauldron of rebirth, adding the ingredients of our life. In darkness, go outside and look up into her cauldron. The stars are the elements of your life. Name them.*
12th Day	*Find a large wooden box or clay bowl at least three inches deep. Place it on your altar and fill with dry sifted sand. On the night before each sabbat, allow your fingers to draw a design in the sand.*
13th Day	*Spells, like nursery rhymes, should be simple—with a rhythm that slips off your tongue effortlessly. "Rain, rain go away..." is perfect. "Let the silver liquid drops that fall from heaven and fall upon my shoulders..." is not.*
14th Day	*Kachinas going home. Where and what is your real home? Can you write or draw it—the colors, the sounds and smells of home are the essence of your being. If it is not to your liking, re-create it.*

The Priestess of Hazel

The Hallows of Hazel

Yvonne—"Hazel branches are used for water divining. In the same manner, Hazel wands are used to divine essence, meaning and value. The way that a Hazel rod or wand is used for this purpose is through a combination of symbolic gesture and proximity. In other words, if one wields the wand as if to cut or penetrate into a heretofore "hidden" realm of understanding, say—the nature of a relationship or the meaning behind an event—the wand will open a way to gain insight into the issue under scrutiny. Then, if the wand is held against the bosom, in the manner of the ancient Egyptian initiate into the Mysteries (arms crossed upon chest), the sense, or total value of a situation will become clear. This is a method that I've tested many times, as I have a Hazel wand and have used it in just this way.

"I was travelling in the Yukon and Alaska when a friend travelled to England and Scotland. While in England, she visited a traditional witch who lived and worked in the New Forest, a man initiated in the ancient tree magic. He made wands from the different trees by culling the twig or branch from the tree at only the right time, during the correct phase of the moon, and by the sacred methods taught him in his tradition. He always obtained permission from the resident tree spirit, or dryad, an aspect of which then came to live in the wand. He then fashioned simple, beautiful wands from the wood thus taken, and offered them for sale with a small hand-printed certificate explaining the quality of the wood and of its dryad.

"Another friend of mine saw one of these wands when they arrived in Canada with the woman who'd been to England, who owned an occult bookstore, and who had promptly put them on sale in her shop. The second friend was so certain that this was the wand for me that she bought it on my behalf. She was right to do so. It was the wand for me, being small, simple, beautifully wrought, and with an operative part that was shaped like a blade. This is an incisive wand, it penetrates to the essence of issues as if it is cutting into clear water. It is made from a slender branch of Hazel, and the smooth, speckled bark is still upon it, having been oiled to a glossy finish. I treasure this implement and consider myself very fortunate for the train of events that led it to me.

"The sense or meaning that one gains from Hazel divination is wholistic and complete, as if all aspects of the situation are simultaneously revealed. This is due to the "merging" or melding property of Hazel wood. Its own inner logic and dynamic is based upon a symbiosis with water, which translates as "meaning," symbolically and elementally. The situation is suddenly rendered into understanding "in the round," or like a spherical model of interacting forces. This phenomenon has to be experienced to be believed so I leave it to you to find or make a Hazel Wand, if this prospect appeals to you."

It is due to these special properties that the Hazel divining instrument confers the ability to adjudicate or mediate in disputes. The insight gained in Hazel meditations is so inclusive that it affords a surprisingly complete and accurate, compassionate and objective understanding of the issue under dispute. One can only be fair in adjudication when entrusted with the vulnerable "truth" of a situation so completely, as by the generous Hazel wood. It is a sacred trust in every sense of the term.

The "Salmon of Wisdom" knew all things in an instant when he swallowed the Hazel nuts that dropped into the stream. This is the quality of the "gnosis" or experiential knowledge that the Hazel divination brings. It is as if realization and enlightenment are suddenly within you and, indeed, have always been there.

Hazel

June 27–July 3

15th Day	*A day to celebrate all the amazons you've met since the end of Holly.*
16th Day	*On white paper with red ink, write a spell asking for Amazon grace. Seal it with honey for the gift is bittersweet. Burn it in your bowl of sand. Fire, earth and air—no water in this spell. Why?*
17th Day	*Under night skies, chant to Cerridwen, listing the elements you would like her to add to your cauldron. Be greedy but promise her your respect in return, she asks nothing more of you.*
18th Day	*Did you find home? Like the turtle, you carry it with you for it is your essence. Wherever you are, you are home.*
19th Day	*Find Witch Hazel and explore her potential.*
20th Day	*Amelia Earhart disappeared on this day that honors expectant mothers. Gossip said she was pregnant. To some of us, pregnancy is spiritually toxic. The Lady blesses you with the wisdom to know and the grace to choose.*
21st Day	*End your week with Cerridwen and her stars like grains of sand, for so are your opportunities and your potential. Hold like sand with open palms, for if you grasp too tightly it will all slip away.*

The Hallows of Hazel

The Totems of Hazel

The Salmon is a Totem of Hazel month, as are an assortment of crustaceans. The exoskeletal denizens of this month owe their significance to the Cancerian quality of much of Hazel. The crab, the tortoise, the lobster, and the scarab beetle are all symbolic of instinctive lunar drives and attractions that are deep and primal. They are also tremendously tender and vulnerable creatures, whose soft inner structures are protected by a hard, resistant carapace.

The crab and lobster inhabit the depths of the sea. They are quintessential lunar creatures, being influenced directly by Her tides. The fathomless deep is their natural home; the watery, emotional realm is their medium.

The Tarot card of the Major Arcana which best expresses this reality is The Chariot. This card is ruled by Cancer, and features a Charioteer, in full armor, guiding a chariot led by two, polarized beasts. In some cases these beasts are horses, in others, they are sphinxes. In every case, one is black and one is white. They each pull in different directions and it is the Charioteer's task to guide them in a balanced, neutral path.

In fact, the Chariot card implies "balanced action" or the need for it. There is a spinning top on the front of the chariot, to signify this gyroscopic balance. This is the "middle path," that avoids extremes, hubris, or arrogance. This is also the mediational ability of the Hazel month, conferred by compassionate understanding.

The Charioteer wears armour, like an exoskeleton. This is like the protective shell of the crab or scarab beetle, and even like the hard beak of the salmon. This armour, like the shell, is the vehicle (or chariot) that enables the vulnerable self to essay into the world without injury or damage. In psychological terms this is the persona, or mask. Within this socially acceptable vehicle, the self can remain safe and undetected in its acute sensitivity and tenderness.

Adopting the Crab, the Salmon, or the Scarab Beetle as an ally for certain tasks or undertakings will equip you with the ability to present a public face without compromising your inner integrity and responsiveness. If you imagine that, like the Crab or Charioteer, you are armoured by an exoskeletal shell that cannot be penetrated, you will find yourself able to remain perceptive, responsive and aware, without feeling vulnerable or exposed. Your inner core will remain protected and function as a guidance system while your persona deals with situations. You will be able to divine the essential truth of problems without becoming overly involved or compromised. The carapace or shell is an essential tool for sensitive natures or delicate situations, for it provides a necessary detachment.

Jessica—"It is probably no accident that my very favorite nut of all is the Hazel; my work largely draws upon my ancestral memories which are rich and varied, combining the gifts of many cultures. In the same vein, my favorite fish is the salmon, a totem of Hazel in Irish mythology. The salmon, according to legend, became inspired with wisdom upon ingesting nine Hazel nuts (3x3, the number sacred to the Lady—and to myself as a triple nine, by numerological analysis).

"Cancer, the zodiacal sign associated with the Hazel month, represents the Mother archetype in contemporary astrology. This is, however, just one of the expressions of the sign. In my experience, Cancerians are among the best travellers, knowing how to take themselves into the greater world. It is as though those of them who travel know their own boundaries and how to approach the boundaries of others, whether they be the boundaries of land, culture or language. Their intuitive abilities enable these individuals to absorb the necessary information which promotes their success in their travels. It would not surprise me at all if there were a preponderance of archeologists and anthropologists (both of which are professions pertinent to Hazel) of the Cancerian persuasion."

The rabbit, or Moon Hare, is a totem of witches, shown in countless folk tales in current circulation in the British Isles, Europe, and China. The "Moon Hare" is a shape shifting magical woman (or Witch) and transfroms into a beautiful maiden, like a moonbeam. An English tale from the oral tradition tells of a village Wise Woman and her wise old horse, who hide a fugitive rabbit from the evil huntsman and his hounds. They are pursuing the little, white creature. The Wise Woman puts the rabbit in her horse's pannier basket. They then stand in the middle of a clear-running stream (a prophylactic against evil) so the huntsman and hounds do not detect them and race by. When the old wise woman opens the basket, a beautiful woman emerges to thank her.

This story is a modern, folk version of the ancient tale of Rhiannon (from the Welsh myth cycle, the Mabinogion). Rhiannon was a Goddess who took different animal forms in which to explore Her wilderness. Hopping along one day, in the form of a white rabbit, She heard the baying of hounds and realized she had caught the attention of a hunter and his dogs. They were in pursuit of Rhiannon and chased Her over hill and dale until She came within sight of a handsome youth. He took pity on Her and scooped Her up into the folds of his coat. He carried Her over a stream, and the hunter and hounds swept by, having lost Her scent. When they had gone, the handsome youth (whose name was Cian) found he had a beautiful woman in his arms instead of a rabbit.

Rhiannon looked favorably upon Her new friend, and they lived an idyllic life together on Her enchanted island, until Cian abused the privilege and raped Her—whereupon She turned onto an enraged Mare, kicking him in the thigh and shattering the bone. Cian was crippled but wiser for the rest of his days.

Hazel

22nd Day	*Be a mountain spirit. Feel the power of wind and air and space. A hill or a cliff will substitute. Mountains, like seas and ships, were once called "she," for they are the breasts of Gaia.*
23rd Day	*In 1851, students rioted to keep women from Harvard's medical classes—I swear by Apollo!*
24th Day	*The bull-run in Spain was a tribute to the goddesses with horns. Why? She never asked for the blood of strong young men. She has no need of it for she bleeds and doesn't die, but lives and gives life.*
25th Day	*Women were kept from sweat lodges and sacred places during menstruation, for men found their energy too powerful. This honesty was refreshing, for other cultures claimed they spoiled the butter and soured the milk. Enjoy your sexual dreams, a gift of the blood moon.*
26th Day	*"His"story proclaims this day the oldest Women's Festival. Wrong. Life is the oldest Women's festival.*
27th Day	*Hazel ends with Hel, the Queen of the Underground and the Dead.*
28th Day	*Fear not the darkness of the Night Sky. Ruled by sleep, she is a mirror image of the dark underground ruled by her elder brother, Death. Just as kind, just as loving and just as forgiving, his embrace will eventually give peace.*

The Totems of Hazel

Vine

S ymbol of the first Harvest and its celebration, Vine represents the culmination of the summer and the first viewings into the oncoming autumn and winter months. He portends a time of divination, as the fruit of the Vine is the grape. Mother of wine, Vine represents altered states of consciousness, as wine alters one's perceptions of the outer, and often inner, world.

Vine brings visions and inspired hallucinations. The fruit of the Vine confers "divine madness," the escape from the round of usual work and pleasure—the "rapture." Transports of elation or despair are not uncommon with this month, so remember to remind yourself that this is simply timely.

Dionysus is the god-form that is most associatied with Vine, or his Celtic counterpart, the Green Man. Pan and various sylphs, nymphs, and faeries are also appropriate here, so if you find yourself hallucinating them, remind yourself that you are probably not mad, it is simply the season for them to make an appearance. Feelings of gregariousness, garrulousness, and generosity are also appropriate here, as well as feeling socially expansive.

Vine is companion to all Soul work, associated with Dionysus, whose followers were largely women. Dionysus' story is multifaceted: he is presented to us as an ambiguous figure, from effeminate to mad to drunken to exalted. He honored his mother, Semele, (who was consumed by the sight of his father Zeus as a thunderbolt). He is also god of theatre, the persona or mask we wear as we move through the mundane world. His constant companion is Pan, whose name gives rise to the word "panic," a state in which all our senses are heightened, rendering us altered.

Dionysus was a vegetation god, the genius of viniculture, and a form of the Green Man. Like other "Divine Sons," his religion was an outgrowth of the worship of the Earth and Moon Mother (Semele) in that any and all religious thought and social, ritual practice began with the concept of the earth/moon mother Goddess. The "Divine Sons" of the Earth/Moon Mother were the archetype of the fruit, and grain Gods (like Attis, Tammuz, Damuzi, and Adonis) born of their mother, the earth, and reaped (or sacrificed) for the nurturance of the tribe, village, and (later) Neolithic city. This was the context of the women's "weeping for Tammuz in the temples" so reviled by Biblical writers. The weeping was a form of ceremonial mourning for the death of the young God who would be reborn in the spring, with the new grain. There was no human sacrifice associated with these rites. If there were, we can be assured that the Biblical writers would have listed this among the "abominations." Human sacrifice was a feature of the service of patriarchal godforms due to a misunderstanding about the "cleansing" power of blood—so obviously referring to menstrual blood, that requires no loss of life.

Agriculture was first developed in the matriarchy and was a central aspect of religious practice. The priestesses of Demeter were the guardians of the seed grain and conducted rituals and composted elaborate concoctions from sacrificed pigs for its fertilization and enrichment. The animals who thrived from a particular type of food crop were the symbol and sacrificial stand-in for the grain or fruit god—the bull in grain-Goddess religions, pigs for the rituals of any vegetable crop whatsoever, and the goat for the rituals of the Vine (goats feed on grape leaves, and the skin of a black goat was used to fabricate sacred wineskins). When the sacred/sacrificial animal of the Divine Son of the earth/moon Goddess was sacrificed (on the eight major harvest festivals of the year) the entire population ate meat—and usually only at these times, so the sacrifice of the animal/godform was gratefully received and considered extremely holy. These rituals were originally conducted by women in their role of priestesses of Semele, which gave rise to the legend of the Maenads, Baccantes, or "Bassarids," as they were called by the Lydians. In later days, as patriarchy grew in influence throughout the ancient world, the cult began to center around the Divine Son aspect of the essentially agrarian religious systems, and Dionysus' rituals were taken over by a male priesthood. Vestigial practices of the wandering "Wild Women" (or Maenads) persisted, however, well into Roman times.

The latter part of Vine corresponds astrologically to the sign Leo, the solar masculine aspect (which sits diametrically opposed to Willow, the lunar feminine). He is a a time of generosity, heart and expansion—a time of plenty. His rituals are those of gratitude and the singing of praises, theatrics, externalizations, and hyperbole. Leo is the sign of the King, the sun and the theatre as well as of children, the "fruit" of the human vine.

As befits him, his leaves are used for decorative purposes.

The fire-holiday, Lammas, occurs in the final quarter of Vine. This festival commemorates Lugh (Llew, or Lu), in the first fruits harvest of the Light God of the summer growing season. It was seen as the time when the God was sacrificed, or harvested. The grain in the field, the corn on the stalk, the fruit on the vine was taken, its light energy reaped for the nourishment of the community. This event was felt to be very holy and gratitude was expressed in offerings made to the earth. This was also a time when the Goddess and the God were perceived to commune in the sexual dance of the Sacred Marriage, and also as a time when the Earth Bride took the life of the son/lover/grain/crop, and translated it into the life of the tribe. Seeds were stored for the coming planting season, and preparations for another turn of the wheel of the year were made.

Vine Rune is Mannaz, the rune of humanity, relationship of one to another, the Sacred Marriage consummated, the fruit of the union, androgeny, the masculine perspective (of partnership, community, etc.), thus reason and logic.

The Gaelic name for Vine is Muin, the letter is M, and the Ogham symbol is shown below.

Rune
Mannaz

Ogham
Muin

Vine

1st Day	*Fete of Magdalene the Harlot, in honor of ladies of the night. Considered to be the greatest prize as wives, they brought experience, compassion, understanding and pride to their homes and family—and a darn good dowry.*
2nd Day	*We think of the clans as extended family and friends. In Vine we find cultures far apart in time and space celebrating similar festivals of women, in all their glorious diversity.*
3rd Day	*Ndlovukaze, the Queen Mother Elephant, is adored with a Reed dance. My favorite joy is to walk like a stately elephant bowing and waving a trunk to friends. Try it. Royalty does it perfectly.*
4th Day	*In Asia, we celebrate O'Ban, similar to Samhain or Halloween. Trick or treat yourself.*
5th Day	*We begin the Celtic time of Lughnasah, the Light of the Vine.*
6th Day	*Carmen, a Roman midwife and healer, bids you feel the energy and life-affirming power of your hands. Hold, caress, or massage someone—yourself, if no one is available.*
7th Day	*Tailiu is the Irish Goddess of the Gateway Between the Worlds. If you are following the rich panorama of women, heroines, goddesses and female milestones, you—as Tailtu—have opened a gate to your rightful heritage as a woman.*

The Vine Tree

The Priestess of Vine

She takes you by the hand and leads you into the fields full with the bounty of the first harvest. As you gaze about you, notice the tall, proud sheaves of wheat, the trees laden with ripening fruit, the vines bursting with plentiful grapes, purple and green and indigo. The dramatic flowers of summer sway enticingly, inviting you to drink in their magnificent colors and fragrances and to marvel at their majesty.

As you stand entranced by the sight before you, your attention is suddenly drawn to a rowdy group of revellers who appear—just coming over a knoll to your left. Their merry-making excites you; you notice a very beautiful young man accompanied by several women of all ages. He is wearing a crown of woven vine, adorned with modest white and yellow flowers. He looks barely more than a boy in age, but his eyes are filled with ancient wisdom. His bearing and manner suggest a man of maturity and confidence. He is obviously the delight of these women who dance in merriment around him, freely and unabashedly.

Out of the crowd of revellers darts a figure; your heart starts to pound as your mind tries to assimilate what it sees. The figure is unmistakably half man and half goat! He continues to dart about, stampeding, roughly rushing at the young man and the women. You experience a sense of panic as you watch him narrowly miss them. This seems to only increase their enjoyment and pleasure and they all shriek with laughter. Then you realize who these people are: Dionysus, Lord of the Vine and his faithful attendant Pan, the All-Father, wildman and guardian of the primal masculine spirit.

As you watch with growing understanding, the merriment suddenly stops and Dionysus drops to his knees, reverently embracing the ground. Your blood seems to tingle as it courses through you. You begin to move almost involuntarily as though to join this remarkable congregation. Just then She takes your hand and leads you into the Temple grove.

The groves were the original temples. The Sacred Groves of Britain, Gaul, Romany, Greece, Jordan, Syria, North Africa, and all parts of the Middle East contained the trees held most sacred in that area. Hebrew maidens danced in the sacred groves, vineyards, and orchards for the fertility of the crops, and the Ashera was the form of the Goddess in her manifestation of the Tree of Life that graced early Hebrew altars. Greek pillars are the stylized columns of trees holding up the roof of the Temple, a stylized sky. In this way, early temples reflected their original form, the grove. The Egyptian temple design often included a room of pillars to designate the forest wilderness where an initiate must wander on the way to enlightenment.

The Maenads, or Bacchantes, danced in the vineyards to bring in and contain the energy of the Wild, and they courted it in the guise of the Wild Man of The

Woods—Pan, Silenus, or Dionysus, the goat-footed god. "Dentrites" means "Young Man of the Tree," and is a title that refers to him as the Divine Son of the (Earth/Moon) Mother Goddess, the literal fruit of the womb. Grape vines were cultivated on T squares, the original form of the Tau Cross, a structure later used by Romans for crucifixion of state enemies. This motif fed the legend of the death of Jesus Christ, as much of the Dionysian myth was absorbed into the Christian myth structure, including the name/title: "Christos," meaning "Anointed One," and also "Son of the Virgin Mother." Dionysus was worshiped by Jews in Jerusalem under his Phrygian name, "Sabazius," alongside Jehova. The bread and wine sacrament of the transubstantiation, whereby the sacrificial food becomes the "body and blood of the god" originally belonged to the worship of Dionysus, in which women went onto the hills in procession carrying a small, wicker basket containing a bread manikin. This was hailed as Dionysus, regaled and honored, then torn asunder and consumed ritually. Later, state-run rituals of Classical Greece required the sacrifice of a surrogate goat, with the first part of the sacrifice rendered to the state. The rest was consumed by the Priestesses and Priests of the God, and the populace.

When the rituals of Semele/Dionysus were taken over by a male priesthood, the priests were constrained to wear female attire, similar to the priesthood of the cult of Attis (Divine Son of Cybele). This is the root of Dionysus' reputation as a cross-dresser or transexual. He was also the patron of freedom and liberty of personal expression, and so was "Pan-sexual," embracing all forms of love and erotic practice.

Vine

8th Day

Nephthys, sister of Isis, shares the duties, burdens and secrets of her sister. If you betray another woman, you betray yourself, for we are one in nature and spirit.

9th Day

Opet, a celebration of love and sexual unions in all their diversity. Do not judge others, expressions of love.

10th Day

A day of bindings. Weave matching bracelets of Vine and link them together for you and your loved one. Wear them in your secret moments. If you are alone, hang them on your bedpost for the future.

11th Day

Maya New Year Stone Year.

12th Day

Mystery and instinct are only part of the myriad descriptions of woman.

13th Day

What is your description?

14th Day

In sunshine, play the games of Lugh. In moonlight, listen for the call of the Raven.

The Priestess of Vine

The Hallows of Vine

With the onset of the Vine month we enter, once again, into the realm of the cup and the blade. In this segment of the Wheel of the Year, we meet the blade as the cutter of bonds, restrictions, and tethers. Also, we prepare to reap the fullness of our efforts and growth. We begin to feel the bittersweet mellow savor of the Autumn of the Year. Vintage and aged beauty becomes apparent, as ideas and fruits gain their maturity. The ideas of harvest and sacrifice are prominent at this time, and the Green Man of the Vine peers from the leaves and ripened fruit, waiting to be taken and consumed. The Maenads feel the call to give, in generous abandon, to the gods of harvest. It is one of the more orgiastic times of year as, indeed, "to everything shall be given a season, and a time to every purpose."

Visionary beauty may stalk you here. You may find yourself the willing prey of pleasure.

Jean—"My search for my Holy Grail, as I called it in my adolescent-romantic phase, was as doomed as the search of Arthur's knights. Sometimes I caught a glimpse of it—silver and crystal overflowing with life-affirming water, the element associated with cups.

"My morning coffee is not as important as the cup that contains it—thick enough to warm my hands, the rim thin enough to feel smooth against my lips and, most important of all, never used by anyone else. The sight of someone drinking from my cup turns me into a neurotic harpy and the cup is immediately banished. At lunch or dinner, any cup is acceptable and I have no hang-ups about restaurant or friends' cups. With this background, I didn't expect my cup search to be easy.

"My altar has bowls and cauldrons, but drinking from a cauldron is frowned on by most covens and straws are really not accepted. So cups, goblets, and chalices come and go—plain or beautiful, glass or metal—they all fail because they are not my cup. My son, Kevan's, Yule gift was a silver wine goblet, the bowl festooned with grape clusters held aloft by the upraised arms and the forward-bent head of a strange creature. Long hair obscured the face and shaggy fur covered legs that ended in cloven hoofs. The naked torso had breasts. Wonder of wonders, it was a woman! I had found my cup.

"Kevan's gift the following year, a silver and crystal coffee server, was discretely returned and exchanged for another goblet, identical to the first. Almost immediately dissatisfaction set in. The bowl was too shallow. Choosing which one to use became a minor crisis; my perfect cup multiplied became a source of angst. The water element represented by your cup is the symbol of your emotions.

"When I see and hear others' emotional response to life I am aware that my response is not as strong. In comparison to others' "love" mine would be fondness. My "anger" is annoyance touched with amusement (except when dealing with a bully, intolerance, bigotry and discrimination). I had always believed that when I found my chalice I would also find my emotions. Perhaps as a young person I drank from too many cups. I never found one that was sweet enough—nourishing and satisfying enough—to say, 'This is right for me; I will search no further.'

"Like the knights of old, I know I will not find my Grail, or my true emotional responses, in this lifetime. But it does not mean that I will stop searching.

"Unable to shop for a suitable gift, I gave the pair of cups to Janet and Stewart Farrar when they visited us from Ireland. I hope the pair of goblets found peace with a pair of witches. Liquids, like emotions, take the shape of their container."

Jessica—"My first chalice was a handmade bowl crafted by a Mohawk friend of mine. It was she who also gave me one of my favorite wands which is made from the stretched phallus of a bull.

"My second chalice, an elegant silver one which I always use during rituals and for my altar, was given to me by a gentleman who was my student at the time. More important even than the beautiful chalice is the friendship that it holds."

Vine

July 25-31

15th Day	*The shadow of Dumballa crosses the land. Male insecurities are exaggerated.*
16th Day	*"All witchcraft comes from carnal lust which in women is insatiable," from Malleus Mallificarum, the Hammer of the Witches, written by two celibate monks, Sprenger and Kramer in 1486.*
17th Day	*"Blessed art thou, oh Lord, our God, that I was not born a woman..." —a Jewish prayer.*
18th Day	*In Belgium a procession of and for witches winds its way down country lanes and city streets. Buy balloons and invite your friends to the park for a parade.*
19th Day	*It is the gathering time for the clans. Create a name and clan devoted to your ideals. Today, gather your hereditary clan for a feast and memories.*
20th Day	*The Mic Mac natives claimed St. Ann as Mother Earth and Goosecap as Father Sky. New history claims Goosecap as a Scottish prince who brought the Knight Templars to North America. The roots of magic run deep.*
21st Day	*Diche Lugnasa, or Lammas Eve. Rejoice in the knowledge of the growing seed within you. It is first harvest, full of anticipation for rewards to come. Contracts are made this day for a year and a day.*

The Hallows of Vine

The Totems of Vine

The sign of Leo colors three quarters of this month. The lion is a creature with a vast body of myth around it, linking Lion to many diverse cultures.

In dynastic Egypt, the lion was a symbol of the impeccability of Pharaoh. The Pharaoh was expected to become a spiritual Adept, and undergo the tests and trials of magical initiation. The battle with the lion was a symbol for the initiatory candidate's mastery of the personal will, and her or his struggle with the powerful, beast nature. When the beast nature was properly and compassionately understood, it became gentle and served the initiate with its great strength.

The legend was that the initiated Priestesses and Priests, which included the adults of the royal family, lived in close proximity to Lions without fear of attack. But if an initiate fell from grace, became duplicitous or false in their stance—in other words, if they lost integrity and were therefore not "impeccable"—the lions would attack and rend them instantly, sensing the victims loss of sovereignty, or command, of Self.

Percival befriended a Lion, who then followed and served him, in his adventures. The story goes like this: Percival was venturing upon his Grail quest, when he saw a "serpent" (or Dragon) pass by with a lion cub in its jaws. He then saw an adult lion give chase and engage the serpent in battle for the life of the cub. Percival decided to support the lion because it was a more "natural" beast. He attacked the serpent and slew it, whereupon the lion befriended him and became his devoted companion.

The lion is a symbol for the sun, or the personal will. This is the fire-nature that lives in the third chakra, or "will-center," and gives the heat of energy and assimilation to the body consciousness. It is like a personal inner sun—an orb of heat and light. The lion and the Sun are also symbolic of the Heart center, as the "risen" sun (or Will-energy elevated to the commpassionate-relationship awareness of the Heart) becomes a new kind awareness— royal, loving, and beneficient. The image of a lion in battle with a serpent connotes the battle of the evolved will with the survival-based energy of the root-chakra serpent energy—the unawakened kundalini. When the lion is befriended and championed, it becomes gentle and provides loving service. Of course, the lion is the serpent, at another octave of awareness. Percival's mythical predecessor, Owein (Yvain in Medieval French romance), fights and kills the lion, thus gaining access to and mastery of the powerful, beast energy of the more predatory, survival-oriented parts of Self.

Lion-headed Goddesses are fierce protectors of The Past and ancient secrets. They stand as guardians of esoteric lore and magic. The portals of primordial memory are protected by Sekmet—the lion-headed Goddess of dynastic Egypt. She preserves occult knowledge from the eyes of the irreverent or profane. One must be impeccable in her or his Will to venture into the remembrance of reality-changing awareness. If there is not complete ethical certainty, one's own inner Sekmet, as Will-guardian, will prevent one's magical progress. This is for the mage's own protection, as much as for anyone else's. When we remember how to effect dynamic change in the world—as a matter of birth-right—it is necessary that our motives have integrity, and that we trust ourselves and our motives completely.

The lion-headed Dakini of the Tantric, left-handed path performs the same protective service. The Goddesses Ishtar, Astarte, and Cybele were traditionally depicted seated upon lions, or drawn by them in chariots. The Lion is also a heraldic animal for Apollo and Christ.

The lion is noble, and family and clan oriented. Lions are concerned with the well-being of the young and infirm, and expect good, social management to provide for this concern. Lions, as predators, winnow the herd of weak or ailing members by preying upon them, thus benefiting the gene-pool and managing population. Within the pride, family roles are defined and carefully exercised as a web of mutual support.

Lions are grand in gesture and in stature. They are expansive, royal and proud. The Lion totem will help you to contact your own "Grand Manner" during this month, as well as your social conscience and tribal organizational skills. Excesses may be likely. Lions do everything with style and magnitude. Generous feelings and magnanimous gestures are apparent, and the savor of life lived fully.

Dionysus' symbolic sacrificial animal was a black goat, called Dionysus Eluetheria ("Freedom") and called Liberius by later, Roman versions of his cult. Another of Dionysus' power animals was the leopard (or panther) and priestesses who conducted the rituals of Dionysus wore leopard skins in some instances. The Bassarids of Dionysus/Semele associated Dionysus with the fox and wore fox skins ritually. Fox gave rise to the innumerable "Reynard" myths and tales about the wily, trickster character. Reynard is wise, cagey, irreverent and usually triumphs. He includes androgynous qualities of Hermes, Mercury, and Dionysus, and has the flowing and changeable qualities of these godforms. Fox is his own authority and in no way heeds external rules but regularly breaks them to his own advantage. Vestiges of the worship of Dionysus' Fox totem by the Bassarids can be found today in many folk songs and stories based upon the exploits of Raynard or Raynardine. An English folk song with French roots describes the making of a Bassarid:

"Oh day and night she followed him, her eyes so bright dear child,
And he led her over the mountains, did the sly, bold Raynardine"

Panther or Leopard, on the other hand, exemplifies the rigor of wild nature, and the necessity of observing Nature's laws above all others, lest She turn, rend and tear. The power of the Wild and the ineffable wisdom of remaining in harmony with this great force is expressed through Panther.

Vine

22nd Day	Lammas, or Loaf Mass, or Lamb's Fair, is the daylight celebration of the craft. Womankind, who planted and tended the first gardens, is hailed as the giver of agriculture and civilization.
23rd Day	La Negrita Women—women on a pilgrimmage for black stones. Where will you find one? Seek diligently and leave an offering upon the stone.
24th Day	Be a dryad, dabble your feet and hands in water. Leave the imprint of you as an offering to the Goddess of Water.
25th Day	Light a balefire, burn letters and reminders of pain. Toast and eat the sweetness of marshmallows and the future. If necessary, use a microwave. Women are the facilitators of change.
26th Day	Visit the wind as an element of air. Sing, howl and roar your pain and joy into the universe as offering and tribute. Earth and water, fire and air, all are acknowledged and honored. See to your soul.
27th Day	Begins a month of ghosts and spirits. Ghosts—dead memories of the past, must be exorcised and laid to rest. Spirit—the indestructible part of you, played many roles in innumerable lives and saved the very best to become the you of today—Lady bless you...
28th Day	All rituals end by moving Widdershins, or against the sun, to let energy go. If your right arm is outside when you turn a corner, you are travelling Widdershins. Take a Widdershin walk at bedtime and sleep in peace.

The Totems of Vine

Ivy

As you wander in the labyrinth you meet yourself at the center. The relentless Ivy is noted for her ability to grow and thrive under the harshest and most adverse conditions. She is representative of the developing Self, her twisting, spiralling growth pattern indicative of the path we all must take in our own personal evolution.

Since antiquity, Ivy has been paired with Holly as a symbol of life in its potency, though too much Ivy in a decoration would invite ill-fortune in the coming year. It was also claimed that to place Ivy under one's pillow would promote dreams of one's true love—perhaps a vision of one's inner Self or masculine or feminine self. In the Greek myth of Theseus and Ariadne, the thread with which Theseus was led out of the labyrinth after his encounter with the Minotaur (his Shadow self) is the same winding Ivy thread which is the measure of his life and Fate, given him by the Weaver, Ariadne, whose name means "most holy."

During our research, we discovered two varieties of ivy: one is English Ivy, member of the Ginseng family, and the other is Ground Ivy, member of the Mint family. English Ivy berries are toxic and so are large quantities of the plant herself. She may be used externally as a poultice for cuts and eruptions of the skin. The bark resin was sometimes used to relieve toothache.

Ground Ivy, according to the old herbals, was used in instances of persistent cough as well as in lung disorders. She was also recommended for flatulence and fever. Doctors used her as a remedy for "painters' colic" (lead poisoning). Undoubtedly she is no longer used for this purpose and her application in the other areas has been under question. She does, however, contain a high dosage of Vitamin C. Ivy is reputed to cause hallucinations and intoxication, and indeed a highly intoxicating ale can be brewed from Ivy. Paradoxically, one of Ivy's benefits is thought to be as a cure for drunkenness. As different parts of the various varieties of Ivy are very toxic, it may be that it was used as a purgative.

Maenads were said to chew Ivy leaves for erotic/poetic frenzy, much as the Pythoness of the Oracle of Delphi chewed Laurel leaves. Both Vine and Ivy grow spirally, a potent invocation of evolutionary growth and resurrection. Ivy was sacred to Osiris, the dismembered, resurrected God. Ivy represents the perennial return of life, creeping into scenes of devastation and renewing them with green, life energy. The Ivy played a female role to the Holly, and their sexual dynamic is preserved in the Pagan carol, "The Holly and the Ivy." The Holly was the male staff or club, the Ivy its encircling "nest."

Ivy seems always to triumph. There is no host inhospitable enough to discourage the thriving growth of Ivy; Ivy can find and maintain a foothold anywhere. One of the most rewarding sights, somehow, is that of an utter ruin crowned with verdant Ivy.

The Ivy brings an understanding of the spiral of the Self—the realization that the journey inward into the subjective awareness, if travelled far enough to the core, links us to the objective perception that is the collective, or Universal, consciousness.

Jessica—"Many years ago I was given a baby Ivy plant as a gift at Yule. She lived happily for a very long time, thriving in her hanging pot which I always kept in my bedroom. Recently I moved to a new house and placed my Ivy in my room, as was my custom. She seemed to adjust well to the move and new location. Then suddenly one day she died. This was curious, since at the time I was experiencing a major transformation and restructuring of my (inner) relationship to my outer reality."

The Rune for Ivy is Gebo, which connotes harmony, gifting, hospitality, contracts and agreements, and sexuality.

The Gaelic name for Ivy is Gort, the letter is G, and the Ogham script is shown below.

Rune
Gebo

Ogham
Gort

Ivy

1st Day	*On the First of Ivy, women in Nepal stop work to celebrate the Goddess within. Follow the example of these very wise women. Declare, "I am the embodiment on earth of the gracious goddess. I am She."*
2nd Day	*Vinalia Rustica, a wine festival honors an urban Venus of love and luxury or a pungent Pan, smelling of musk and decaying leaves. Your choice.*
3rd Day	*As meteors and shooting stars illuminate the summer sky, redefine your aims. Changes in work, education, and friends are coming.*
4th Day	*Puck Fair—dress in boyish clothes and with your female friends enjoy a night of playful masculinity.*
5th Day	*List the things or actions that made you feel masculine. What was your strongest trait or emotion? Did you enjoy the evening?*
6th Day	*Today give apples to a friend who reminds you of Diana, and place garlic at the crossroads for Hecate.*
7th Day	*Secretive Ivy covers massive walls but while it changes from summer green to winter red, air roots are tunneling into brick and mortar. Castles and monuments are destroyed by this small, inoffensive plant.*

The Ivy Tree

The Priestess of Ivy

Find yourself a picture of the Milky Way and one of the helix and place them on your altar. Study the spiralling pattern they portray. Trace the spiral into and out of the centre. When you have finally achieved an understanding of the spiral motion, experience the sense of the spiralling of your own DNA, the foundation of physical life.

The spiral is a sacred symbol, a sacred dance, a sacred motion. It represents, among other things, a journeying inward to the core of the essential Self, the dwelling place of the Mysteries.

Prepare to journey: traditionally, such a journey is undertaken with the aid of a Priestess. Choose a time when you will not be distracted or disturbed.

Create a sacred space where you will bathe and purify yourself. Light white candles and burn a purifying incense such as sandalwood or frankincense. As the bath water runs into the tub, sprinkle in a handful of salt and bless both the water and yourself. Enter the bath and feel the cleansing power of Earth (salt), Air (incense), Fire (candles) and Water. When your purification rite is completed, pull the plug and stay in the tub until all the water has drained away. As you emerge from the tub, evoke your inner Priestess and ask her to guide your spiral journey into yourself. It is important to secure her aid in this process. If it is not the right time to journey, She will indicate this. Respect her judgement; this is her territory.

Under the instruction of your inner Priestess, create a sacred space for your journey to commence. When the space is prepared and the Circle is cast, envision a labyrinth with your mind's eye. As you stand with your Priestess at the entrance, pick up the ball of thread which you will find lying at your feet and give the loose end of it to her. As you walk into the Labyrinth unroll the ball. This is your way back out.

In the Labyrinth you will encounter a manifestation of the Weaver. She may appear to you as Spider Woman; Arachne (an aspect of Athena) the Three Fates; The Wyrrd Sisters; or the Three Faeries. The Weaver is Guardian of our Fate (i.e. our genetic code) and Mother of our Rebirth. Allow yourself to be tutored by the aspect or aspects that you meet. This knowledge is a sacred gift. You may ask questions, though you may not always receive answers to them right away.

When this interchange is complete, you may decide to continue inward still unrolling your ball of thread or you may return to your waiting Priestess, rolling up your thread as you go. The choice is yours. Remember to thank those who have helped you (the Weaver and the Priestess). Record your experiences in your Book of Shadows.

Your journal, in which to record your dream life and rituals, can be your cherished confidant during this month. Think of such a journal as a kind of mind-map of the inner landscape. This journal is called the "Book of Shadows" because it is a record only, and any record is but a "shadow" of the "real thing."

Ivy

8th Day	*The air roots of Ivy burrow into your carefully constructed Wiccan and Goddess belief system. If you are to leave the path of Wicca, it will most likely be in the month of Ivy. Fault finding and doubt cause many students to abandon their search for the Goddess.*
9th Day	*Later, too proud or embarrassed, they never return to their Goddess search, which is really a search for themselves. Some thought it would be easy or instantaneous. Is Ivy testing your dedication?*
10th Day	*The potential for transformation, the magic wand, is and always was yours. The Goddess and Witch is already within you and has been through all time and space. You must find her and set her free.*
11th Day	*Any so-called "women's work," properly done, expresses some aspect of the Goddess, for she has a form for every function.*
12th Day	*Queen Isis, during her search for Osiris, served as house slave and nurse to the infant sign of a minor queen. She was not diminished or demeaned by seemingly menial tasks, but came closer to her goal.*
13th Day	*With Beltain as planting time, you have passed your first trimester. What are your feelings? What actions or directions will you take? Does your creation grow well and properly?*
14th Day	*You are travelling the labyrinth of your mind, turning this way and that and then doubting yourself, retracing your steps. Now you, like Isis, face a challenge. The reward is more hard and joyous work, loss and gain, and answers that bring more questions.*

The Priestess of Ivy

The Hallows of Ivy

Yvonne— "When I lived in New York, I underwent a serious illness, and something happened to my psyche that was like a loss of any and all ego defenses. I was at the mercy of all of the emotional injuries that I'd suffered throughout my life, yet had been in denial of. All at once, they swept over me like an inundation. I had to acknowledge how hurt, furious, and grief-stricken I (in truth) was—and the realization shattered me.

"I was involved in an assortment of therapies. I was under the care of a nutritionist-chiropractor team, a masseuse, an aromatherapist, a polarity masseuse, and a rolpher. I had regular meetings with various counsellors. I also participated in a healing circle for several years. My program of healing was, in short, intensive. I was completely broken down and it was a good time for these healing arts to get past my defenses, as I had none.

"During all this, and while my magical development was progressing apace with the healing going on (which is the only way it can work, I am convinced) I felt the need to acquire the right Chalice, as a vessel or container for the emotional content that was being released in my psyche. There was a certain colour of light that accompanied my forays into the watery realm. This light was actually a kind of guide. I was reminded of the "HooLaLoo, a super-intelligent shade of the color blue" from Douglas Adams' *Hitchhikers' Guide to The Galaxy*. In actual fact, it is common for people to have a perception of brilliant, blue light in the third eye with regular meditation, and this roughly describes my experience of it.

"The blue that I saw was a deep aquamarine, or turquoise light. It had an electric quality, and a mercurial activity, like quicksilver. It was tremendously magnetic—a kind of "conscious" light.

"One day, while passing the jam-packed antique store between my apartment and the laundromat, I peered in the window to see a large blown-glass chalice of exactly that type of blue. It glowed with the clarity and tranclucence I'd come to expect of my blue light, and I knew it was the perfect cup for my altar, and for the conscious containment of my reclaimed, true emotions. I purchased it, not quibbling over the price, which I think surprised the proprietor somewhat. I have it still, and cherish it."

The cup and the blade are the tools of this month. The blade here observes its function as harvester, culler, or reaper. This is when intellectual activity can help you to define what is of value to you—what you choose to keep, and what you choose to discard. Attachments or habits that are counterproductive or outmoded can be trimmed, with conviction, from your life now. There may be a poignancy to such decisive action, but there will also be a sense of rightness and of timeliness. This is where you can sacrifice the grapes to make the wine.

Ivy

15th Day	*Trust your instincts. The way out of the labyrinths is intuitive. Place your doubts in the lap of the Goddess; if you listen, she will answer in your own voice.*
16th Day	*Vulcan lights his fires; Juturna and the Goddess puts them out with water. Your choice: will you be fire or water or the steam they create?*
17th Day	*The Mundus Ceresis pit is opened to let the souls of the dead visit us. Visit them in a library or museum.*
18th Day	*Write a letter to your great, great, great grand-daughter. Tell her who or what you were.*
19th Day	*Some call the Craft a cult. A cult is defined as having a physical being, living or dead, as its head. This describes many belief systems, including Christianity and some forms of Buddhism, but it does not describe the Craft.*

new Moon

20th Day	*A religion is defined as having a spiritual being as its head or leader. The goddesses and gods of our craft are a composite, representing female and male spirituality. The Craft is a religion, philosophy, and way of life.*
21st Day	*Archaic men placed their gods where they felt fear and awe; gods who were bribed with gold, jewels, and blood.*

The Hallows of Ivy

The Totems of Ivy

The Wolf and the Spider are the guardians of the month of Ivy. According to Classical Patriarchal Greek mythology, Spider was once a beautiful young woman named Arachne, gifted and skilled in the art of weaving. In a contest with Athene her excellence in her craft was clearly evident. However, because her tapestry depicted the amorous exploits of the deities, she incurred the wrath of the Goddess and so was condemned to an eternity of spinning and weaving as a spider.

The story has much older roots than Classical Greece, however, and Athene is a Goddess much older than Patriarchy. She is related to Metis of Lybia, and is herself a form of Arachne. The Spider, like the Owl, is a totem of the Goddess as Weaver of Destiny (the Owl suggesting Her dark, oracular and transformative aspects). She is also featured in Celtic, Native American and African mythologies as a creative deity or force. Her story of weaving, creating, holding and enclosing can be found in the mythologies of peoples all over the world. Thus she is a symbol of our connectedness, the strands of her web transferring the slightest vibrations between us all, a constant reminder that everything we do affects others. Seen in sunlight, the spiderweb reveals itself as prismatic, running the spectrum of color from red to violet, and every color in between. The Spider's web is symbolic of the warp and weave of all, crystalized, earthly possiblilities, whereby potentialities are made manifest. The spider is Mother Maya, spinner creatrix of the physical world—the interference patterns of energy, her loom.

Jessica—"The Spider is one of my personal totems, travelling with me from childhood. I have always had a particularly strong interest in her as well as in her relative, the scorpion (both are arachnids). I experience the spider as the creative, expanding aspect and the scorpion as the wary and possibly self-destructive aspect, as the scorpion is known to sting itself to death if frustrated. The creative aspect turned against itself can indeed become self-destructive, collapsing in upon and finally devouring itself."

The theme of weaving and creating extends to the creation of the Self, and the weaving of aspects of our innermost being to create a cohesive Soul. The story of Ariadne, Goddess/Priestess of ancient Crete, illustrates such a journey. Once again, patriarchal Greece gives us the story of Theseus, an Athenian youth whose task it was to destroy the Minotaur, the bull-headed off-spring of Pasiphae the Moon Goddess. The Minotaur dwelled in the centre of a great labyrinth, built by the master Daedalus. As the story goes, Ariadne led Theseus to the Labyrinth where she presented him with a ball of thread, telling him to unwind the thread as he made his way into the labyrinth and to wind it back up again to enable him to find his way back out.

Traditionally the work of priestesses has included the preparation and guidance of those who would undertake a journey into the Underworld (or Otherworld), what we may now refer to as the unconscious (which does not preclude the possibility of the numinous experience or travelling into the Void or Dreamtime of ancient legend). She would await the return of the traveller and would help in the assimilation of the hero(ine)'s experience.

Theseus desired to overcome his animalistic (bull-headed) instincts (astrologically ruled by the moon) and so sought the mediation of Ariadne to enable him to go into his lunar depths and to return to solar consciousness. The rest of the story suggests that, although Ariadne performed her duty, Theseus was unable or too impetuous to fully integrate the experience.

The Wolf is the guide to and the guardian of the Underworld. Wolf can guide you on your Westerly journey, into the realm of intuition, dream-vision, and emotion. The lands of the Unconscious are safely entered and negotiated by the offices of the black dog or wolf guide, and the great Goddesses and Gods (Primary Energies) are approached by Wolf's introduction. Wolves are the totem creatures of Lupus Diana, and of Hecate. Wolf can gainsay any troll, ogre, or demon under any bridge, mountain, or tree along the Path, and is a devoted and loyal Ally.

Jessica—"Though we hear of the 'lone wolf' (and certainly my own experiences of the wolf have been with the singular variety) this dignified being is a symbol of loyalty and family devotion. In order to have something to offer others, however, one must first have a sense and surety of self. Wolf in the Native American tradition is associated with the Teacher, the keeper of knowledge and companion of the moon. The Dogon people of Africa and the ancient Egyptians held that the Dog Star, Sirius, was the home of the Gods. The dog is the relative of Wolf and represents such aspects as service, friendship and guardianship. There are many tales about Wolf nurses of human heroes. One such story is of Romulus and Remus, the twin brothers who founded what became the city of Rome. Their legendary beginnings tell of the brothers being cared for by a she-wolf.

"Not all stories of the wolf present such an amicable picture. The Fenris wolf of Germanic and Scandinavian myth was the devourer of Creation, anxiously awaiting Ragnarok, the Twilight of the Gods. As the devourer we see reflected the destroyer aspect of the Goddess, the grave which devours our physical form, transforming it into soil. Beyond Ragnarok is the new (or renewed) Earth. These are times which see us transforming ideologies and concepts which we have long lived by. In order to recreate a more equitable existence, each of us must follow the lone wolf of self and allow the outmoded to be devoured to give way to the new."

Ivy

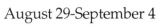

August 29-September 4

22nd Day	*Women found their goddesses where there was love and laughter. The Goddess requires no gold or jewels, for everything is Hers. She needs no blood sacrifice, but only your devotion.*
23rd Day	*Charis—a day of mercy... Ann Hutchison was banished from Massachusetts for criticizing the Christian ministry in 1730. You may criticize the Goddess and yourself, for you are one.*
24th Day	*Anata — Time of the purification of your Kundalini serpent sexual energy. How? By indulging or abstaining, of course. By your choice.*
25th Day	*Feast of first fruits. Plan a day of vegetarian delights. Try to live and eat in the season.*
26th Day	*You are the finest of fruits of her garden. You are a miracle and a gift to the world.*
27th Day	*Lakon—A healing festival for maidens of the four directions. Heal your wounds by removing the thorns of cruel, unkind or unthinking words. Healing will follow.*
28th Day	*Mayan boundary day. Make a pilgrimage to the borders of your everyday world. Choose the parts you can and will live comfortably with. Expel the people and situations that keep you from happiness or fulfillment. Buy a pot of Ivy and train it in a circle. Plant your joy within.*

The Totems of Ivy

Reed

M oses, Heracles, Perseus, Oedipus, Jason and many other heroes were hidden by their mothers in the Reeds and drawn from them in a magical rebirth, or initiation, by their magical foster mothers (a version of the fairy godmother).

This initiation is actually the penultimate stage of the year-cycle threshold. This is the period of time when all the momentum and content of the previous part of the year requires only direction and intent to be brought to fruition in the form of realization, enlightenment, or more material results. The dynamic of Reed is like that of a well-aimed arrow, driving home to completion, resolution, or definition. The action of Reed is that of the timely master stroke, or perfect expression of an intent.

The Pike fish, which remains concealed in the reeds until its targeted prey is in clear sight, then darts out swiftly and directly to seize it, expresses Reed energy very well. The pike doesn't move until the time is exactly right. Then there is no hesitation, but swift, efficient, well-placed action. There is no wasted energy in aimless activity; care is taken so as to have perfect, calculated aim. Then success is assured, without striving or effort. The momentum of the well-aimed intention flows effortlessly home to the objective or desire, for it is impossible for it to go awry.

Jessica—"Though the Yew tree (symbolic of immortality and rebirth) can also belong in this position on the Sacred Wheel, many feel this place to be held by a variety of the Rush family, the Reed. The Reed reminds me of bullrushes,

169

bamboo and pampas grass, that tall and graceful white-haired plant that dances in the autumn breezes.

"In all cases, Reed and its apparent relatives feature long and slender shafts, reminiscent of both pea-shooters and flutes. The pea-shooter as a "weapon" affords the advantage for the hidden or distant aggressor. Many's the time I recall being the victim of some hidden boy's dried pea-bullet on my solitary walks home from school or my mother's errands. Usually he was too far away for me to be able to deal with him directly; I would have to plan a counter-attack, as my family expected me to "stand up for myself."

"The flute as a musical instrument is dependent upon the direct action of the player's breath and fingers for the transformation of wind into music. Whether weapon or instrument, both uses identify Reed with direct action and contact. Astrologically, Reed is associated with the sign Libra, the military strategist as well as the artist and negotiator, balance being all-important to the outcome of a given situation.

"There are many myths and stories in which the hero is either hidden among the bullrushes or set adrift upon water in a basket made from rushes. The Reed's or bullrush's affinity with the water element is well-known as the plant grows at the edges of rivers. Here the theme of remaining invisible or hidden until the appropriate moment to emerge is emphasized. One may go so far as to say that the success of a venture depends upon the emotional maturity of the subject, or upon action(s) performed at the ripe (mature) moment, intuition playing no small part in the decision."

One way to marshal energy and wield it consciously is to name it. A name is a word that, when aimed with care, can shape or render a thought or desire with precision.

Jean—"Primitive religions believed we consist of a Physical Body, an Astral Body, a Shadow, a Soul, a Heart, a Spirit or 'Ghost,' a Power, and a Name— seven aspects of Self and a Name, like a ribbon, to tie them all together. This explanation satisfies me as a woman and as a witch. I know my Heart and my mind are frequently at odds, and that my Astral Body does rescue work on the astral plane whilem my Physical Body sleeps quietly in my bed. A part of your Shadow, like a memory, remains bonded by light to whatever earth it touches. The 'Ghost' or Spirit, called a Khu, obtains its life from negative energy and emotions. It may remain active after death, tied by emotional energy to places, people or things. Your Power, like your talents, remain with you always—used and acknowledged or not.

"What is the name of your Power? Do you aknowledge it? Do you use it wisely? Do you command it or does it command you? If you do not know the name of your Power, ask the Goddess. She will tell you, in a dream or a thought. When you have your Power's name, you will know your own, true Name."

The Autumnal Equinox, Alban Elved, occurs about the middle of Reed month and the sun enters Libra. The hours of day and night are again equal at the Equinox and there is a balance and harmony of lunar and solar energies. From this point the hours of night exceed the hours of day and will continue to do so until the Vernal Equinox. It is an ideal time for rituals of inner balancing.

The Rune for Reed month is Ingwaz, signifying potential, yielding to a greater power, Mystery, DNA, the double helix, and corporeal intelligence.

The Gaelic name for Reed is Ngetal, and the letter-sound is Ng (pronounced 'Ing'). The Ogham symbol is shown below.

Rune
Ingwaz

Ogham
Ngetal

Reed

1st Day	*The month of Reed, rooted in earth, body bathed in water or emotions, and face upraised to air, mirrors the passage of Reed month. No matter how firm your feet are on the ground, your body remembers the near and distant path.*
2nd Day	*A witch is a witch—young or old, male or female, we are all called witch. It is not necessary to declare this publically or to wear its signs unless you so desire. It may be more efficient to be silent.*
3rd Day	*Many of us reply, when asked, "I don't worship the devil, if that is what you are asking."*
4th Day	*Taking the title, "witch," is a vindication of those who have died, accused of Christian heresies, among other things. But it is not a "comfortable" title. It is defiant of the oppressions of an aeon.*
5th Day	*Clean your altar for all of the fire goddesses. Pele likes orchids and gin.*
Full Moon	
6th Day	*Public witches find it difficult to sponsor many mainstream causes for their presence may alienate others. If you support the S.P.C.A., zealots will say you want the animals for sacrifice.*
7th Day	*Current fear and ignorance decrees that your motives may be misunderstood. Together we might change this.*

The Reeds

The Priestess of Reed

You arrive at the Temple of Athena, Goddess associated with martial arts, strategy and negotiation. As you pass through the portal, you notice much warrior-like activity; fencing, archery, and various forms of target practice. In a corner of one room an instructor stands in front of an attentive group describing the principles of negotiation, the art of winning without either party being compromised. You stand and listen to her inspired speech for a moment, wondering at this paradox. How does one prepare for war and peace simultaneously?

You are distracted by a Priestess gently but firmly taking you by the arm. You have been so engrossed in your own thoughts you did not hear her approach. The two of you exchange knowing glances; she caught you unawares, unprepared. She may have been a stalking aggressor. You make a silent note to yourself to be more alert in the future.

The Priestess leads you into a small room where you find a short, white tunic waiting for you. She instructs you to change your clothes, to assume another role for your stay here. She then leads you into the Temple garden where you join a group clothed like yourself taking turns aiming a weapon at a target; some have bows, some have spears, some have blow guns. You are instructed to choose a weapon and make a choice. The Priestess addresses you:

"You have come here to learn about targeting. In order to move in a direction, you first have to know what direction it is. This is an exercise in achieving a goal. For now, the goal is a bull's-eye, but later you will learn how to set goals for yourself in life. We work here within the context of the group to enable you to form an understanding of your responsibility to your community and also because a joy of personal victory shared enriches us all through inspiration and encouragement.

"Be true to yourself and to your goal. Know how to focus and to take aim. Only in this way can you activate your potential and be of value to your community, which is the world."

After your sojourn in this temple, retire to a place in your mind for target practice. In this place, take a bow into your hands. This bow is the shape of the year so far. Then take up an arrow; you are going to weight and trim this arrow, with feathers. The arrow is your intent, and the feathers are any fine points or qualifications upon your intent. Then, in your mind's eye, see yourself taking careful aim at a bull's eye target. The center of the bull's eye is your goal, whatever that may be. Now see yourself take careful aim. Hold the tension in the bow string for a moment, until you feel the precise, right moment. Now loose the arrow, and see it fly absolutely true to its target, the bull's eye. Repeat this process whenever you think of it.

Reed

8th Day	*At the "Virgin Fair," men decreed that only inexperienced women may dance the tratta. The Goddess bids all to dance. Nurse Edith Cavell executed as a spy this day.*
9th Day	*Today we light the fires for nephthys and the spirits of the dead. May they see our everlasting love and respect.*
10th Day	*The days grow shorter and the lunar nights are dark. Our time of rest is coming. Make every day count.*
11th Day	*Asormos, the gathering of the initiates of the Eleusinian mysteries begins. Do you truly seek the wisdom of the ancient ones? The wisdom is yours. You have always known the secrets for you are a woman.*
12th Day	*Holade Mystai—bathe in the sea and don new clothes. Are you ready to release yourself from this life and sink into the earth and sleep and dream? Will you rise again tomorrow as the blades of wheat and barley?*
13th Day	*Offering of barley and grain to Demeter. Be warmed by the fire of the sun and of love for both are a gift of the goddess, Eurynome—endless and everlasting as her love for you, for you are her child.*
14th Day	*Prepare a holy basket for Ceres. In it place grain and flowers, a mirror, a comb, and a snake, symbol of rebirth, knowledge, and sexuality. Stand firm in the wind, for inside it you will hear the voice and words of the lady. In its embrace you will feel her love.*

The Priestess of Reed

The Hallows of Reed

The work of the Blade is varied. One of the functions of the Blade is to cut obsolete or regressive tendencies from the Self, and to pare and trim outdated circumstances from one's life. The Blade works with the medium of Time in interesting ways, due to its quality of opening portals and inaugurating new possibilities and realities.

Jessica—"When I first decided to externalize my commitment to the Path after my second initiation, I felt it was an appropriate time to acquire my first blade. Looking within and asking for guidance, I received the information that my blade was to be a copper and oak one (which I later learned was a tool of a Northumbrian Faery Tradition of Witchcraft—a Faery tradition being one that traces its roots to the oldest races who occupied Britain).

"I knew of no knife makers other than a group who operated in Ontario. I wrote to them for their catalogue and finally sent them my request and payment. They assured me that they were working according to the proper lunar and astrological timings in the manufacture of this instrument. Despite my patience, I never did receive the item nor a refund.

"My first blade was purchased in the camping department of a store in Montréal. It was a plastic-handled (fake bone) hunting knife and served its purpose well for me for about four years. Just at the time when it was no longer appropriate, I was "called" into a knife store in Victoria, B.C. After a grand tour of the entire store, which featured many fascinating items, I was about to leave, disgruntled at not having found anything pertinent to me, when suddenly I looked up to see *it*. My beautiful blade was hanging on the wall right next to the shop entrance, a copy of a commando knife. When the staff member placed it in my hand I was elated. It felt so perfectly suited to me and remains my very favorite athame to this day.

"However, when a request is put into action, one must expect its fulfillment at some point in time. One day a former student of mine presented me with an oak-handled copper-bladed knife which she had made specially for me. It is a treasure, coming from a friend and reaffirming the eternal vigilance of the answering Universe."

The activity of the Blade in Reed month is that of pin-point accuracy and exact identification of meaning. It is also significant of efficient, direct action with no wasted motion. The Blade of Reed would represent a part of the mind, in tune with the senses, that would watch and wait, and when the time was right, would hone in on an accurate "naming" of the thing or dynamic under scrutiny. As such, it would represent the power to have control or mastery in a situation by bringing the ability to analyze and define the locus, or hub, of its dynamic.

Reed

15th Day	*Heton Lampadon Heaera is a torchlight parade of initiates searching for Persephone. Chilled by the silver rain of heaven, take Persephone's hand. She will lead you through dew clad fields to the rippling, endless sea of her mother's love and joy at your return to her embrace.*
16th Day	*Initiation born of the earth warmed by the fire of love, cooled by the rain of reason, inspired by words on the wind—will you dedicate yourself to the goddess and to her service? Declare, "I am witch and I am woman, I am woman and I am witch. Let no one deny my rite."*
17th Day	*At this feast of maiden mother and crone, take your place in the circle of women and prepare for the great and final test. Are you prepared? "She cuts the cane and reaps the grain, while autumn fruits surround her."*
18th Day	*At the equinox, a time of solar and lunar balance, join the spiral dance of life. Life is the greatest test and the greatest gift. It is yours with love from the Goddess.*
19th Day	*Seek a Plemo Choai, an earthen vessel in the shape of Demeter's womb to hold your secrets.*
20th Day	*You may feel elated, betrayed, lethargic, or any one or all of myriad emotions. Remember, you have died, been reborn, and are experiencing post partum all at the same time. Keep careful notes in your journal.*

new moon

21st Day	*How will you celebrate Sedna, the Inuit sea and underworld goddess? The variety and worldwide devotion of women to their goddesses delights and inspires me. An Inuit pie and a candle is easier to find than the ingredients tradition requires, and she will be grateful.*

The Hallows of Reed

The Totems of Reed

Owl and Pike are Totems of Reed. Both of these creatures hunt with a single-point focus of consciousness, and dive upon their prey with a direct, far-seeing accuracy. The owl sees in the dark and silently aims herself at her objective, materializing out of the gloom swiftly and without hesitation. The pike waits until a hapless minnow is within his sights, then darts out from his shelter of Reeds to take it. Both mean sure, swift death to their victims, and as such are the Reaper in a merciful manifestation.

Initiation is called the "second death" or the "mystical death," for it denotes a transformation so complete that your present expression "dies" and a new expression (of Self) is born. Some of the metaphors for this death/rebirth phenomenon are; the gaining of the "perfect," "light," or "crystal" body. These terms suggest the adamantine, or eternal, Self, beyond duality, death, or decay. When the Witch identifies with the consciousness expressing itself through the body, glimpses of past and future lives (as well as alternative lives) are gained. This is a sense of the body that can travel interdimensionally, as well as in time and space. The Witch, like the Shaman, has the ability to journey in many realms, or "worlds."

A quality, called "impeccability," is the special attribute of the initiated, or adept. This simply means that the Witch shows no hesitation when she sees that a thing must be done. She trusts her instincts and intuition, and the evidence of her senses, implicitly. She trusts her motives, her ethics, and her intent. She trusts her Self. She gives herself absolute authority to *act*. Then her gesture is swift, true, and merciful. She does not doubt herself, nor indulge in self-recrimination or indecisiveness. She is as sure and true in her focussed action as the Owl hunting by night, or the Pike targeting his objective.

The Owl is the power animal of Lilith, Athena, Metis, Mari, Hecate and Diana. Owl is a manifestation of wisdom, and associated with the "Wise-ones" of myth and legend. Merlin is imagined to have an ever-present Owl upon his shoulder, scrutinizing events along with him. The "wise-old owl" is such because of her all-seeing eyes and her absolute lack of hesitation to act when the time is "ripe." Lilith has an Owl form, as well as a winged serpent form— or dragon manifestation. Her earliest appearance seems to have been in Mesopotamia. A carved plaque from about 2,000 BCE depicts Her naked, with Owl's wings and feet. She had a dual role; that of bringing men either to death or to sex, as their bride. In either regard She was swift and merciful, gathering men from the streets for the sexual rites of the Temple as the "right hand of Ishtar," or coming in the night to gather souls to the Great Mother's womb, once again, in death.

The so-called "Eye Goddesses" of old Europe are representations of the Owl Goddess. A later genus of the Owl Goddess, Mari, is seen in the Assyrian

177

figures, with huge, black-rimmed, staring eyes. The many figures of this type that have been unearthed stand in a formal gesture and are robed as priestesses and priests. They seem to guard a threshold, on the other side of which lies the unseen, causal world.

Reed

September 26-October 2

22nd Day	*A day of rest and restoration. Be at peace, for on this day you may safely erase from your life any acts and deeds you well and truly regret. Do not act hastily.*
23rd Day	*On the day of Medusa, the goddess of knowledge, whose face culd turn men to stone, Rachel Carson published* Silent Spring, *a book to melt the stone hearts of those who would devastate our mother earth.*
24th Day	*A few more golden days to harvest each and every gift of summer. Begin preparation for the dream time.*
25th Day	*Nemesis inspires you to seek your true fate. Fill bowls with purple flowers in her name.*
26th Day	*Meditrinalia, a day of women's medicine and healing.*
27th Day	*Durga, mother protector of Bengal. Women know—they may slander and rend your body but they cannot touch your immortal soul for it is safe within the Goddess and you shall be avenged.*
28th Day	*Druidic feast of the guardian spirits ends the month of Reed. You are rooted, bathed and inspired by the blessings of the Goddess.*

The Totems of Reed

Elder

Jessica—"Elder holds dominion over the thirteenth month of the lunar year. I see her as sister to Myrtle in this function, both plants associated with endings and completions. In Classical and North American systems, Myrtle equates in function with Elder.

"Elder marks the last of the harvest, a time of stock-taking to ensure survival over the barren, winter months. It is also a time of honoring the ancestors, of aligning ourselves with their legacies and of divesting ourselves of their weaknesses, their traumas or limiting beliefs lingering in our genetic memories. Thus, it is a time of sacrifice (acts of making ourselves whole). For me, this has always been a time of personal withdrawal and renewal, when the circumstances of my life allow for it.

"Both Elder and Myrtle foretell of transformation, often through death or love. Mythologically, Myrtle is associated with Venus and was often included in the bridal wreaths. Myrtle, being an evergreen, speaks of love everlasting beyond the grave. In the myth of Venus and Adonis, the Goddess of love bargains for her dead lover with Hades, who agrees to return Adonis to the upper world for the Spring and Summer portions of the year on condition that he return to the Underworld for the Autumn and Winter months.

"For three weeks before I met a meaningful love, who lived on Myrtle Street, I sat with my own death. During the course of our association, I made a shamanic journey to the Underworld, to "bargain" on his behalf. The entire experience left me transformed in my views about love, my life, and myself. In Greek myth the Priestess, Myrrha, was transformed into a fragrant Myrtle tree by Aphrodite to shield her from the too ardent advances of a suitor in order that she retain her self rather than be 'consumed' in the fire of another's passion.

"In my research, I have come across three different plants which each go by the name of Myrtle: Myrtus communis; Umbrellularia california; (Oregon or Pacific Myrtle); and Vinca minor (Myrtle aka Lesser Periwinkle). The first variety has been used as an antiseptic, astringent, and as a compress for bruises and hemorrhoids. The second, a member of the Laurel family, as a pain reliever for headache and rheumatism. The third, a member of the Dogbane family, contains substances which reduce blood pressure and staunch the flow of blood.

"Elder and I share a long history. Some of the finest homemade wine I have ever tasted was made from her berries. In my years of living in the bush, we had a small Elder tree in our vegetable garden. My husband and partners decided to expand the garden one year and uprooted the Elder, despite my protestations. In remorse, I planted my infant son's placenta on the spot where she had been growing. Shortly after, my family and I left for a vacation in Eastern Canada. That was in 1974. Though it was meant to be a brief trip, we were involved in a near-fatal car accident which changed the course of my life. I have not returned to that property since, even though we still retain twelve of the original ninety-three acres."

The Elder month is the corridor. This period of time is the link whereby the material and awareness of the preceding year is composted into energy that fuels the new. The powers of death/rebirth are omnipresent here, as powerful guardians of the mystery of personal transformation and resurrection. Metaphorically as well as literally, death is the great transformer. The release of energy into new forms that occurs at the death of an idea, outworn pattern, or organism is transfiguring. Those who are gifted with the "Sight" actually see this as a brilliant burst of light being released.

Elder month is a threshold month; in fact, it is *the* threshold month. The retrospective view is entirely appropriate here. Most of Elder is in the influence of Libra, but will move into Scorpio near the outset of the final quarter. Balance and Judgement in the Aegis of Maat, then a healthy composting of retrogressive waste-energies in the influence of Scorpionic Hecate are likely, even desirable. These are powerful Goddesses. They are the Witch's patrons par excellence and there is nothing to fear from their inspiration.

Elders were considered "Witch Trees." They were thought to actually be the Wise Ones in repose. It was considered the height of folly to axe an Elder without gaining its permission. The "Elders," or elder clan-members—the "Wise Ones," were believed to occasionally take up residence in an Elder Tree as a "Dryad."

The Elder Rune is Raido, signifying journeying, putting things in order, the travels of the sun across the sky (through the Zodiac), priorities, and shamanism.

The Gaelic name of Elder is Ruis, the letter is R, and the Ogham sign is shown below.

Rune   Ogham
Raido   *Ruis*

Elder

1st Day	*Irish folklore reveals a dark reputation for the Elder Tree. Elf or Sidhe arrows were made of Elder. These tiny slivers caused grave infections, ending in amputations or deformities.*
2nd Day	*Careless people who fell asleep beneath this tree awoke totally insane. Do not fear. These stories are only to remind us to treat both tree and month of Elder with proper respect.*
3rd Day	*Spend an hour with Sophia, goddess of women's wisdom, in silence. Her symbol, the dove, graces the Tarot ace of cups.*
4th Day	*Wash your hair in aromatic herbs in honor of Zapopan, the rain goddess of Mexico.*
5th Day	*Do your feel the changing energy as the lunar retires in deference to the solar, hunter energy of winter? Drink sage tea for changing woman.*
6th Day	*This is the first day of the Celtic fading time. Let fear fade from your life.*
full moon **7th Day**	*Hopi green squash dance to hasten ripening for frost is near.*

The Elder Tree

The Priestess of Elder

This is the threshold month. As such, it is the brink of initiation into the adopted path of the Wise. This is a matter of choice and is between you and your own spiritual agenda. Only you know when or if you will make the decision or commitment to call yourself "Witch."

Jessica— "Having been a solitary practitioner for most of my Witch life, I understand how the question of initiation could perhaps be considered a thorny one. For the most part, modern-day adherents to the Craft self-initiate, according to outlines set forth by various writers or by their own inner promptings, both of which I have done.

"A consideration, of course, is whether or not initiation is necessary to one's own purposes. For some, a truly heart-felt commitment may suffice; for others the ritual of initiation serves to make a statement to one's community of one's intent, and to make a bid for the community's support of one's decision.

"For others yet, initiation states one's commitment and serves as an acknowledgement of one's acceptance of the Path and all that it entails. Not the least of the obligations initiation brings is the responsibility for one's own Shadow-self and the dedication of oneself to public/community service.

"Traditionally, the time that an acolyte spends with her teacher is a year and a day (one lunar year of thirteen twenty-eight-day months = 364 days + 1 day = 365 days) before she is initiated into the coven. During that period of time, the aspirant has the opportunity to learn about various aspects of the Craft and to try things for herself. As the Craft does not solicit nor seek converts, no pressure is exerted upon any individual who, after spending time in training, decides not to become initiated. Most who seek to follow this Path do, however.

"If one has been working with a teacher, sometimes it is necessary to seek another teacher. This, too, is a respected choice."

If one has been working alone, by consulting one's own inner wisdom or written lore, then one may decide that self-initiation is premature, or unnecessary. These are all valid choices.

This season is a threshold in many ways. It is the border between the seen and the unseen, the inner and the outer, the living and the dead. Imagine that you are in the precincts of a great, ancient Temple. As you walk through the Temple fields, you watch the activity around you—priestesses are gathering and bundling the dead stalks of plants and debris, piling them onto beds for burning. Here and there bonfires dot the field, flame reaching into the black night sky.

Preparations are being made to honor the ancestors; the Temple stores have been replenished for the coming winter months which ensue after this Holy Day, the celebration of the New Year, Samhain. You approach a bonfire. Its extreme warmth confronts you, contrasting the winter chill at your back. You stand at the bonfire, your face growing warmer and warmer, almost burning with the heat. When the heat becomes unbearable you suddenly turn around. Instantly your back warms up and you face someone you recognize. You haven't seen this person for so long and yet they haven't changed. In fact they look better than ever. You are at a loss for words and the other person smiles at you, putting you at ease.

As you look around you realize that many more people have come to join you. It is then that you recognize a common link between all these people: they are all dead. Yet here they are, all looking alive and well. It slowly dawns on you, the veils between the worlds have fallen away and you are privileged to view into the Otherworld and to communicate with its inhabitants. It is apparent that all is well with your departed loved ones. No vision or tale of torment, eternal flames nor damnation. Everyone looks content and so happy to share this time with you. You are overcome with a sense of awe and deep emotion. Your loved ones smile upon you, sharing a blessing among you all. You start back to the Temple to set a place for your loved ones and ancestors. Tonight you will dine together; it is Samhain, All Hallows Eve.

In many traditions of witchcraft, death is considered the ultimate initiation. Respect for those who have passed over is expressed in the many festivals of the dead that are observed around the world. In Mexico, the dead are regaled with wreaths of flowers, food, drink, masque, music, spoofs, and revelry. There is an affectionate mockery of the "ultimate leveler" who comes to the lofty and humble alike. This annual rubbing of shoulders with the "Reaper" is healthier by far than the bizarre silence built up around the subject in our culture.

Imagine that you approach the river Styx, across which lies the land of the dead. A barge awaits you. A draped and hooded figure stands in the prow. This is your guide to the Otherworld, and will ferry you across the river and back for only one, copper penny. As you approach the other shore, your very substance begins to change and become more ephemeral and "light." By the time you reach the other shore, you have become pure consciousness—able to travel in any realm and return at will. What is here? What cities, landscapes, vistas? Are there people you have known — people you will yet know?

Elder

October 10-16

8th Day	*It is time to glean the fields of your summer. Have you harvested all the joy, love and learning experiences that were offered to you?*
9th Day	*Thesmophoria, a three-day ritual reaffirming woman's rights in honor of Demeter and Persephone, her lost child. Go deep into the earth of your being and bring forth the secret offerings you have made this year. Examine them carefully.*
10th Day	*Nesteia—men must provide their own nourishment, and women must set them free to do so. It is women's honor to provide nourishment for themselves and children. This ancient rite is most appropriate in today's world.*
11th Day	*Kallengenia—in honor of Demeter's sacrifice, end her three-day fete. Examine the offerings that you brought from the fertile darkness within. Are they what you wish to offer the coming year? Re-inter only those ideas that will not deprive you of your goddess-given right to love and abundance.*
12th Day	*Where gaudy flowers bloomed, dry stalks of ripened weeds remain, stately and proud in their tattered beauty. Place them on your altar, for they are a symbol of all women. Our beauty and dignity is endless; in our end is our beginning. So mote it be.*
13th Day	*Freya, whose chariot is drawn by cats, commands, "Feed and care for my faithful friends for winter is coming. They will serve you as faithfully as they have served me."*
14th Day	*On this day in 1916 Margaret Sanger opened her first birth control clinic.*

The Priestess of Elder

The Hallows of Elder

A Witch has no Bible, no "Great Book," to which she or he attempts to adhere. A Witch trusts her own inner voice, conscience, soul-guidance, and the evidence of her senses. Experience is of great value to the Witch, and a record of magical and mystical experience and perceptions is kept in a personal journal called the Book of Shadows.

The Book of Shadows records dreams, spells, poetry, visions, revelations, thoughts and theories. It is a recipe book, diary and time-keeper. In the Book of Shadows are recorded rituals and Sabbats, moon-cycles and astrology, numerology, runic messages, Tarot formulae, or whatever personal divinitory information you may want to record. Stories, lyrics, drawings, designs... creative expressions ideally should fill a Book of Shadows, for this is the "bible" of your own journey—your own ongoing creation.

Jessica— "I once had the opportunity to meet with one of my teacher's teachers. During our brief but effective session, I had the experience of standing in a doorway with my back to the "Fields of Light." (Ed. note: This is a sensory hallucination of the "Inner Planes," or "Light Realm" of causality that magical practitioners sometimes experience. Dione Fortune has written extensively about this.)

"So bright was the Light that I could 'see' it through the back of my head! I knew that if I turned around, 'I' would be absorbed into the magnificent Light and 'I' would cease to exist as an individual entity. In front of me I was aware of a 'sea' of humanity; those closest to me looked beautific, their faces beaming, illuminated by the Light. As I looked farther back I became more aware of the murmur of the crowd and I could see strife and struggle in the darker regions.

"Suddenly my consciousness moved from my body and positioned itself slightly to the left of the crowd. When I looked toward my body, I saw only a Shadow framed by Light. I resolved then, as a Teacher, to always remind my students that what they learn from me is only the Shadow, not the Essence of the Teaching.

"Everyone dreams, and yet there is probably no other language or experience that is more personal and individual. Your dream symbols are yours alone although to say this does not deny the fact of the Archetypal (prototype) dream which is a reflection of the collective unconscious, the subconscious pool of human experience proposed by the psyche-logic explorer, Carl Jung. Dreams have many faces: they can be precognitive, forseeing the future; they can be recurring or thematic; they can be informative, healing, amusing; they can be terrifying "nightmares" which some ancients saw as messages from the realms of the Goddesses.

"Dreams know no boundaries, therefore are not limited to our "waking" experience of a three-dimensional world. Dreams can also be the shortest distance between friends. I met my "dream brother" after dreaming of him (and he of me) for many years. We recognized each other instantly. Friends have often appeared in dreams to give me information which they had omitted or forgotten in waking life.

"Much has been written and recorded on the nature of dreams and dreaming including the famous children's song, "Row, Row, Row Your Boat." A favorite story tells of a holyman who dreamed he was a butterfly. On waking he wondered whether he was a man who dreamed himself a butterfly, or a butterfly dreaming himself a man.

"In keeping a dream journal as part of a Book of Shadows, the first rule to remember is: not every dream needs to be interpreted. It is important to notice how you feel upon awakening. Make a note of this. If you choose to analyse a dream, write down your dream immediately. You may also record your dream using a tape recorder. Voice-activated recorders are excellent for this purpose. If you record your dream on cassette, take the time later to transcribe it. Writing the dream down helps the process of recall and interpretation and provides you with a reference table. Always date your entries. As you look back at the record over the years you will notice how you have continued to "work" the details of your dream. Dreams are a living language."

Elder

15th Day

Walk the night, feel the tingle of anticipation. Is it joy or is it fear—or is it both?

16th Day

The great horned fair welcomes Herne the hunter, whose stag-horned head haunted the dreams of women. It was ever thus, in the deep recesses of our soul we remember the wild huntsman.

17th Day

Bettara, the sticky sticky fair, in honour of Ebisu, god of good luck. Celebrate as you will. We shan't touch this.

18th Day

A kite festival for boys in Japan, but why not you? Or someone you know? Fly mental kites, if nothing else.

19th Day

The veil between this world and the next becomes thin and we can hear the voices of the dead on the wind. Do not fear, death does not change their love, care and concern.

20th Day

Belini and Hecate bid you tend the crossroads of your life and choose your path wisely.

21st Day

Feast on bread and grains. Bake with fruit of harvest. It is time to tend the graves.

The Hallows of Elder

The Totems of Elder

The Crane, Stork and Ibis are symbols of the flight of the spirit, its migration in the unseen realms, and its return to a new incarnation. The sight of a Crane or a flock of Cranes augered a death or a birth, depending on whether the Cranes were coming or going. The old wives' tale that storks bring babies is rooted in this mythic significance.

Cranes were considered by ancient Britons to be the repository of mystical moon wisdom. When the tide was low, the treasures of the Crane Bag of the Irish oceanic God, Maananan, were not to be seen. But when the tide was high the treasures were made visible. The "Crane Bag" was made from the skin of a woman, or a shape-shifting Crane Priestess. It held the magical secrets of the Druids, including charms, incantations, language, stories, myths, poetry, Ogham script, and Runic symbols. The "Crane Bag" is actually the term for the collected wisdom of the Druidic Adept.

Cranes were deemed very holy due to their solemn, ritualistic approach to mating, or to war. Their dances of love or of aggression are so subtle, intricate, and aesthetically expressive that the Celts studied them for symbolic language, out of which grew the Ogham shapes. The shifting patterns of their long legs during flight were the basis of the Seer's divination of the transmigration of souls.

The Egyptian Goddess, Maat, is the model for the Zodiacal concept of Libra. The Tarot image of "Justice" is also based on this paradigm of fairness and scrupulous judgement. Maat weighed souls against an Ibis feather, to gauge their burden and determine their path of transmigration. In this office She was aided by Thoth, Her male counterpart. Thoth has an Ibis head, and is an air deity. He corresponds to Mercury and Hermes, and is the God of Magic. Ibis feathers have great magical energy and confer the ability to discriminate wisely.

Thoth is the God of the Crossroads, as Hecate is the Goddess of the Crossroads. As such, He governs movement, communication, transmutation, and travel. His personality is like Papa Legba of Vodoun, or Loki of Norse paganism. Hecate is one of the aspects of the Goddess that we countenance at this juncture of the year. She is in Her Crone aspect, but with the rejeuvenated maiden aspect shimmering just below the surface, ready to emerge.

There is a short, enigmatic Scandinavian folk-tale about a farmer who was working in his field, bringing in the harvest. He was working very hard, trying to harvest as quickly as he could. A large stork flew over and stood close to the farmer, watching his every move intently. The farmer became nervous, thinking the stork might attack him or give him a sharp peck. Finally the farmer got so unsettled he flung his knife at the stork, wounding the bird slightly, whereupon the stork grabbed the knife in his beak and flew off squawking.

After this the farmer became obsessed with the idea of travel and migration. He put down his hoe, left the farm and travelled the four corners of the world. He went to Africa, Asia, all parts of Europe and the New World. Often his compulsion to travel was a hardship to him. He thirsted in deserts, sweltered in jungles, and was seasick on transoceanic voyages. He ended up in Egypt one year, and complained to the landlord at the inn about his dilemma of having to travel continually ever since he flung the knife at the stork. The landlord listened to all he said, then left the room for a few minutes. Then he returned and showed the farmer what he held in his hand saying, "Is this the knife you speak of?"

The farmer was amazed and said, "Yes! That is my knife alright."

The Egyptian landlord then said, "I tell you, I was so angry when you threw that knife at me that if I hadn't raised fourteen children on your barn, I'd have pecked your eyes out."

This story illustrates the lineage of the idea of Thoth, the Egyptian psychopomp and conveyor for the transmigration of souls.

Jessica—"Along with the Wren and the Raven, the Crane was held most sacred by Druids. Many Celtic heroines assumed the shape of the Crane. A symbol of parental devotion because of the extreme care she will lavish upon her young, the Crane is also a warrior bird whose elaborate mating dance, one orthinologist suggests, is a way to abate the natural aggressiveness common to both sexes. Once mated, Cranes maintain a life-long bond.

The Crane as totem implies a personality which is at once graceful and fierce. In Celtic mythology she is associated with transformation and divination or oracles, and is companion to the Lady of the Lake.

As the Ibis-headed God, Thoth was associated with the transformative powers of the moon, though eventually with the advent of patriarchal thought this role was allocated to a woman named "Woman-Light of the Shadows— which suggests a lunar/subconscious function (as Thoth was also a psychopomp, a conductor of souls to the Underworld). He is also the God of the hermetic tradition of Magic."

Elder

1st Day	*Honour Lilith, defamed by Judeo-Christian myth as a soulless monster because she refused to be subservient to her husband, Adam. Find her real story.*

new moon

2nd Day	*Leave gifts for the (faery) Sidhe, on the doorstep tonight. A saucer of milk will do.*

3rd Day	*Margaret Sanger's first birth control clinic was closed and she was arrested for distributing obscene material. Now that's really obscene.*

4th Day	*Owagit, Hopi women dance to celebrate the squash in the vine. Carve a pumpkin and dance with him in your arms.*

5th Day	*Isia—rejoice! Isis has found all but one of the parts of her dead husband and lord, Osiris. Her search is over; she may rest.*

6th Day	*Iroquois celebrate the feast of the dead with memories of heroes and ancestors.*

7th Day	*Angelitos—the Toltec god, Xite, presides over the feast of the dead children. He is the patron of goldworking. Give candy wrapped in gold to children in remembrance of the forgotten little one who died unnoticed, of poverty, abuse and neglect.*

The Totems of Elder

The Day

The Day coincides with the thirty-first of October (unless it is a leap year, when the solar calendar makes up for lost time). A synthesis of lunar and solar time is achieved every nineteen years, by astrological systems. Nineteen is the number of the Sun in Tarot, and describes the number of solar cycles that transpire before the two systems collude, keeping the significant days, or Sabbats, in their proper placement upon the Wheel of the Year. The Day is All Hallows—known to many as "Halloween." To still more people the world over it is known as Day of The Dead (Mexico), All Souls' Eve, Hallowmass, All Saints' Eve, and by many other names that commemorate the dead. The significance of this day in many societies is that of death/rebirth and, as such, it is an initiatory passage. The "Mystical Death" is an aspect of every transformational process, and a feature of every transcendent/ecstatic experience. It is an archaic and vital part of Shamanistic traditions all over the world.

On this Day, be aware of your personal totem as your "ally," and personal guide. This is whatever totemistic guide you have most resonated to, who has most helped and assisted your Path. The Day is given the blank rune, "Odin," signifying unlimited potential, wide open possibilities, the blank canvass on which to paint, the sum of all totalities. The Ogham symbol is Koad, —meaning Grove, and signifying the sum of all knowledge, past, present and future. These are shown below.

The Blank Rune   Ogham
Odin   *Koad*

The candidate for Shamanistic initiation into the Path of The Wise stands at the threshold of transformation. The initiate is forever changed by this experience, and thereby inherits her or his "crystal," or "eternal" body. This is the body that expresses in absolute fidelity the script of the spirit. Some call it the "light" body. What this actually signifies is the moment when the magical practitioner ceases to identify with the temporal and mortal self, and begins to identify with the essential Self, which never dies. In the process of re-identification, and re-integration, the practitioner becomes conscious of this eternal Self, no longer fears death nor even regards it as such, but instead gains access to volumes of soul memory and the power of choice in possible futures. The symbolic death of initiation marks the end of the manner in which the initiate has lived her or his life previously.

The temple initiates of dynastic Egypt underwent a symbolic death, during which they were actually buried alive for a period of hours or days. After this time they were retrieved from the initiatory tomb and considered resurrected. Worshipers of Attis in pre-Christian Rome observed this concept in a ritual procession, carrying an effigy of the dying God tied to a tree in sacrifice. Then the bound effigy was buried in a tomb for three days. On the third day, He was disinterred and declared resurrected. Ancient Celts had a group, yearly process of observing the death/rebirth of the sun during the winter's solstice in barrow grave type temples. A single ray of the sun would penetrate the tunnel grave on a certain trajectory on the solstice, to illuminate a stele, or stone menhir, marking the moment of the sun's re-emergence into increase. In primitive societies the world over initiates into Shamanism undergo a mystical death/rebirth type of trance-journey, including the elements of dismemberment and re-integration, in which they gain all of the magical tools they will then use as a healer and practitioner of the magical arts.

These tools consist of power words and gestures, symbols, poetic correspondences and significances, songs, stories, and the names of specific allies and guides, among other things. In the process of observing the moon-realms of inner-space and the stories entailed in this book, you have already been collecting symbolic tools and mythic awareness. All of these inspirations, and more, may come your way if you are prepared and ready to undertake Self-initiation at this time.

196

Imagine that it is near sunset, and that you walk toward the Hallows Gate of Samhain. How does it appear? Build the image in your mind of the gateway between the realms. Can you see through it, or is it veiled?

You carry in your hands a basket with leaves of all the trees of the year within. As you approach the gate, you perceive that there are actually three gates—that two more gates lie beyond, and three flights of stairs. Still further, you perceive that a corridor, a kind of dream realm, links Samhain to Beltane across a swirling abyss.

The first gate radiates with the colors of autumn leaves, from maroon and scarlet through all the shades of orange, to the pale yellow and beige of early winter. Pumpkins, apples, plums, root vegetables (called Demon Fruit by the ancients) bar your path. The unbearably sweet smell of ripeness overwhelms your senses. Call upon the knowledge imparted by one of the leaves in your basket. Place this leaf among the sacrifice of autumn fruit and step through the first gate.

How do you feel? You see the second gate clearly now. It is made of corn stalks and vines woven into huge animal shapes and cages that change and re-form in the flickering light of the setting sun. Your nightmares, as shadows, move within the rustling, creaking bars. An overpowering smell of decay and vegetation clogs your senses. Instinctively, you reach for the wisdom of another of the leaves within your basket. You touch the vibrations surrounding you with this leaf, invoking the powers of the tree, and the cages ignite. The flames burn away the cages that confine, the nightmares that hold you prisoner of your deepest fears.

As the flames subside, the final gate is revealed. Slim, ghostly Birch trees stand as sentinels on each side of the final stair. White trunks like the fey Whiteladies, branches and twigs like fingers reach out to welcome you. Smoke as fragrant as incense forms a curtain that stretches across the last stair. Glowing embers and sparks like shooting stars light your way in the black darkness of a moonless night.

On this special night, the veil between the worlds is thin, and those brave or wise enough may travel freely, protected by the wisdom of another of the leaves within your basket. If you wish to accept this boon of the Goddess, place your last leaf on the stair and enter freely, knowing that you are entering the dreamtime, where your dreams and intuition will reveal wondrous truth and wisdom, both bitter and sweet. It is your choice. Whatever you decide, may you blessed be.

The Day

October 31

*"All Hallows, one day
choosing of the Witch's way
inward spiral, changing moon
corridor and mystery run
transformation, changing earth
initiation and rebirth…"*

The Tree of Knowledge

Appendix A
Anatomy of Ritual Form

I. Close the Circle: Mark out the perimeter of the sacred space of the working circle by drawing it, making a ring of votive candles, fabric, cord, salt, sand, or by describing its shape in the air or against the ground with the point of your blade or wand.

What this accomplishes is a delineation of sacred Time and Space, traditionally called "A Time that is not a Time, and a Place that is not a Place" where disbelief, doubt, or anxiety are suspended and everything and anything is possible. This is a protected time/space where the deep mind and feelings have permission to emerge and "play."

II. Invoke the Directions: (Use a compass or a map to determine the directions.)

A. Turn to the East and address it with these words (or something like them): "Spirits of the East, Elements of Air, Blade of the Mind, intellect, the Dawning and the Word, Come to me (us), enlighten me (us), bring me (us) inspiration, logic, and design. Grace my (our) circle. Be Here Now. Blessed Be."

B. Turn to the South, say: "Spirits of the South, Elements of Fire, Wand of the Will, Heat of Desire, Come to me, Inspire me, bring me Enthusiasm, Initiative and Courage. Grace this circle. Be Here Now. Blessed Be."

C. Turn to the West. Say, "Spirits of the West, Elements of Water, Chalice of Love, Dreams, Vision and Emotion, Come to me, Fill me, bring me Wisdom, Divination, Gnosis and the Knowledge that surpasses Understanding. Grace this circle. Be Here Now. Blessed Be."
D. Turn to the North. Say, "Spirits of the North, Elements of Earth, Pentacle of Manifestation and Magic, Guardian of the Wild, Come to me, Empower me, bring me Mastery of Function and Form, Strengthen my Body, deliver to me the blessings and the wisdom of your realm. Grace this circle. Be Here Now. Blessed Be."

What this does is acknowledge and bring to conscious awareness all of the aspects of Self. They are made present and accounted for, and can now be focussed and brought to bear on the matter(s) at hand. This process also locates you on the planet, orienting your Self with the currents and forces of the World Self.

III. Turn to the center of the circle. Address the Goddess and the God as the polarities of energy inherent within you. Say, "Lord and Lady, Light and Dark, Yin and Yang, Seen and Unseen, All That Is — Abide within me, Unite within me, Grace this circle. Be Here Now. Blessed Be."

This centers you. The focus is turned inward, upon the eternal Self, and locates you in the position of the "Spinner," the expression of Self that can and does change reality.

IV. Raise Energy. This can be done in a number of ways. You can dance, sing, do deep breathing or chant. You can visualize a spiral Cone of Power — energy from the Earth — revolving around and through the Circle and yourself, sweeping you up into its momentum, and rising to the stars. You can simply sit quietly and meditate upon what you are about to do, your reasons, your feelings, and your expectations.

The purpose of this stage of the ritual is to generate emotional fuel and raise your commitment level to your magical Working.

V. Perform the Empowered Act, the symbolic act that is the point (and the heart) of the ritual. This may be brief and potent, or elaborate and leisurely. The Empowered Act may be a very simple enactment, depiction, or verbal statement of your purpose. The only crucial aspect is that you give it your utmost concentration and believe in it utterly.
A. When this is completed, say,"The Thing is Done. So Mote It Be," or "The Thing is Done. So Be It (And So It Is)."

The purpose of this concluding statement is to affirm that the Work is indeed accomplished and will manifest.

VI. Now take a moment to **contemplate what you have wrought.** See it as profoundly manifest in your life. Express gratitude and ground yourself and the energy you have raised by placing both palms upon the floor/earth. Allow the remaining energy to flow back into the earth, from whence it came, leaving you relaxed and calm.

    A. Eat and drink. Whether working alone or with a group, this is the moment to "commune" with the substance of the world and the profound interaction that is all of life by ingesting food and imbibing liquid. This can be bread and wine, the Witches' **"Cakes and Ale,"** or fruit and water. Taking sustenance into your body both revives your physical and spiritual energy after your recent outlay of vital force, and completes the job of grounding you. (Note: If passing the Cup, or chalice, around the circle in a group—there may be those present who want to participate in the sacrament, but are uncomfortable with the beverage being imbibed — if it is alchoholic, for instance — or with the sharing of "microbes." It is a good idea to give people the option of passing the cup with grace, by giving it a symbolic kiss and then passing it on, or by raising it to the "Gods," then passing it on.)

VII. Open the Circle.

    A. Release the energies that you have evoked from yourself and invoked into the circle by beginning in the North. Release the four directions and their elemental forces, one by one, in reverse order from that in which you invoked them. Face the North and say, "Spirits of the North, Elements of Earth, Powers of the Body, the Natural World, Magic and manifest form, Great gratitude for your many Blessings. Hail and Farewell. Blessed Be!"

    B. Now face the West, and say farewell to the energies, using the same word-formula. Repeat this process with the South and then the East.

    C. Release the Goddess and the God. Say something like, "Lord and Lady, Mother and Son, Shakti and Shiva, Shadow and Light — Eternal Dance of Creation, Abide within me (us), Let me (us) move in your dance. Great Gratitude for the many Blessings. Hail and Farewell, Blessed Be."

    D. Open the Circle by saying, "The Circle is open, but unbroken. My (Our) work is done. So Mote It Be," or the traditional, "The Circle is open but unbroken. Merry Meet, and Merry Part, and Merry Meet Again."

This act brings you back to "normal" consciousness (Space/Time) putting essential ego walls and filters back in place so that you may negotiate your way in the world safely and comfortably.

Appendix B — Tree and Totem Chart

Tree	Totem	Astro-Sign	Traits	Dates	Rune	Ogham
Birch	Snake & Eagle	Scorpio ♏	Celtic New Year Renewal, Transformation	Nov. 1 - Nov. 28		
Rowan	Horse	Sagittarius ♐	Astral Travel Witch-tree Protection	Nov. 29 - Dec. 26		
Alder	Raven	Capricorn ♑	Wealth, Power Stability, Form	Dec. 27 - Jan. 23		
Willow	Bee & Dove	Aquarius ♒	Female Light, Organization Fertility, Sun Moon (Brigid)	Jan. 24 - Feb. 20		
Ash	Dolphin	Pisces ♓	Sacrifice, Intuition, Compassion, Resurrection	Feb. 21 - March 20		
Hawthorn	Stag & Unicorn	Aries ♈	Cleansing Preparation Purification	March 21 - April 17		

Tree	Totem	Astro-Sign	Traits	Dates	Rune	Ogham
Oak	Cow & Bull	Taurus ♉	Hinge of year (Beltain) Stamina, Generation	April 18- May 15	⋈	⊤
Holly	Swan	Gemini ♊	Warrior, (Lugh) Lightening Bolt Valor, Hero Male Light	May 16- June 12	↚	⊤
Hazel	Tortoise, (Crustaceans) & Salmon	Cancer ♋	Creativity Essence Insight-Wisdom	June 13- July 10	⋁	⊤
Vine	Lion	Leo ♌	Harvest, Fruit Prophecy, The Clan (Lammas)	July 11- Aug. 7	⋈	⫝̸
Ivy	Spider & Wolf	Arachne ⊕	Spiral of Self Labyrinth	Aug. 8- Sept. 4	✕	⫫

Tree	Totem	Astro-Sign	Traits	Dates	Rune	Ogham
Reed	Pike	Virgo ♍	Direct Action Timeliness Accuracy, Aim	Sept. 5-Oct. 2	⋈	
Elder	Crane, Ibis, & Stork	Libra ♎	Death, Rebirth Journeying, Transmigration of Souls	Oct. 3-Oct. 31	ᚱ	
The Day	Personal Ally	Libra/Scorpio ♎ ♏	Initiation (Samhain)	Oct. 31	Odin's Rune	

Appendix C

A strology

Astrology is an ancient language of the stars (Gr. Aster = star; logos = word; legein = discourse, to speak). Called "the basis of all intellectual life," astrology was formulated in Mesopotamia as long ago as 2500 BC. Throughout the history of science and philosophy, scrutiny of the stars has been practiced by the likes of Pythagoras (531-? BC), Plato (429-347 BC), Ptolomy (100-178 AD), Paracelsus (1490-1541 AD) and Metrodorus of Sepsis (106-43 BC), among others.

Although popular history creates the impression that the field of astrology was largely dominated by men, more thorough research reveals that the art was traditionally considered the domain of women. This is not surprising as "prediction" in general was, and for the most part continues to be, considered a womanly art. The astrologer-priestesses called the "Chaldeans" created the methodology of star-watching as a method of predicting patterns and trends. These priestesses utilized a lunar-oriented astrology to predict appropriate times for planting and harvesting and were able, through careful measurement, to foretell celestial phenomena such as eclipses.

Modern astrology has attracted a fair number of male practitioners, possibly because it is so compatible with its younger sister, psychology (Gr.: Psyche= Soul, breath of life). Psychology-based astrology is called Humanistic Astrology and has been widely popularized by Dane Rudhyar, Liz Greene, and others. Astrology is also highly compatible with medicine as a predictive and preventative tool. Two current leaders in this field are Eileen Nauman and Ingrid Naiman.

There are many other branches of astrology, eg.: Horary Astrology— literally "astrology of the hour," used to answer specific questions, and Mundane Astrology—the astrology of world affairs. As human potential becomes broader and the human experience more complex, the parameters of astrology, too, will grow to accomodate expanded consciousness.

In concert with the moon observations you will make while following *The Witch's Book of Days,* you can become acquainted with some of the practical uses of astrology by acquiring an almanac, a book which is designed to aid you in determining the appropriate times to undertake various activities—such as planting, weeding, trimming your hair, etc., according to the phases and sign-transits of the moon.

Horoscope

Also called the Nativity, the Horoscope is a representation of the planetary configuration at any particular moment, usually at the moment of an individual's birth. The Horoscope is calculated by an astrologer and then interpreted according to the sign, position and relationship of the planets to one another. The relationships between the planets are called aspects—which can be harmonious or challenging. Harmonious does not necessarily mean "good," nor does challenging mean "bad." Challenging aspects are often those which offer the individual opportunity for evolution or growth, and while harmonious aspects may indicate ease, they may also show areas of lethargy or uneventfulness.

What most people call horoscopes are "popular" astrology, based on the twelve, solar signs of the Zodiac, or sunsigns, and usually give a very superficial "prediction" for the day, week or month. Still these hold a lot of appeal for many people, astrologers included, who read them for fun or to see how close a general prediction is to a more thoroughly considered one.

When you read your sunsign horoscope in a newspaper or magazine, also read your rising sign if you know what it is. For example, I read Gemini first, then Virgo for elaboration on my sunsign. In order to determine what your rising sign is, an astrologer must know what time you were born, as well as the location and date of birth. This information is usually available from hospital records.

Find out what your time of birth is, then invest a few dollars (usually between $2.00 and $5.00) to have a computer-generated print-out of your horoscope. Now you are ready to begin exploring the statement made by your own birth. Suggested reading includes: Stephen Forrest, *The Inner Sky;* Demeter George and Douglas

Bloch, *Astrology for Yourself;* Debbi Kempton-Smith, *Secrets From a Stargazer's Notebook.*

The Zodiac

The Zodiac (Gr. Zodion, Zoon = animal) is an "imaginary" belt surrounding our solar system through the middle of which we perceive the sun's "path" during the course of the year. The Zodiac is divided into twelve signs, each consisting of 30 degrees (or 1/12 of 360 degrees). As we, on planet earth, revolve around the sun we experience each of the twelve signs for approximately 30 days. The signs of the Zodiac are: Aries the ram; Taurus the bull; Gemini the twins; Cancer the crab; Leo the lion; Virgo the virgin; Libra the scales; Scorpio the scorpion; Sagittarius the centaur; Capricorn the sea or mountain goat; Aquarius the water bearer; Pisces the fish. There is evidence that there was once a zodiac of thirteen signs, each of 28 days duration, but that one of the signs was dropped—that being Arachne, the spider. It may have been that the sign of Virgo was once two signs, Juno-Athene and Arachne, characterizing the months of Vine and Ivy, for the archetypes of Athene and Arachne are aspects of the same Goddess, connected in myth and ritual, and perceived by some in the night sky. But Arachne, here, would have been in her mighty aspect, corresponding to Metis or Maya as Great Mother, at her loom at the hub of the Cosmic maze, spinning the created world into being.

The zodiacal year begins at the Vernal Equinox, roughly March 21st, when the sun enters Aries. Because the actual year is slightly different to the one observed by the Julian Calendar, the day of entry into a new sign of the zodiac varies from year to year. A book of planetary charts called an ephemeris can tell you the actual day, year to year, that a sign changes. The two to three day discrepancy in sign change is commonly known as a "cusp," suggesting a blending of qualities of both signs under consideration. Each sign of the zodiac has a story, or myth, associated with it. Because, in North America, we are largely under the influence of the Greco-Roman experience of time, our myths are rife with the concepts of these predecessors. Those of us whose heritage is other than European have different mythologies to tell the story of the stars. For example, Gemini is usually associated with twin brothers, often Castor and Pollux, also called the Dioscuri. In some versions, one twin was black and one was white. In others, one twin was mortal, the other immortal. Such was the bond between these two boys that when Castor was mortally wounded, Pollux beseeched Zeus to allow him to share in the fate of his brother. Thus the brothers alternated in their residence of Olympus and Hades, moving from one place to the other every day. In Hindu myth, however, Gemini is considered to be a pair of lovers, man and woman, so expressing polarity and exchange of energy or vital current, but with sharing and intimacy, both strong Gemini traits.

Research and appreciate the mythologies associated with your sunsign. How do the traits emphasized by the myths vary from culture to culture? Which do you relate to most strongly? Suggested reading includes: Liz Greene, *The Astrology of Fate* and Geraldine Thorsten, *The Goddess in Your Stars.*

Numerology

In order to facilitate an understanding of the different energies of the numbers, the following is an explanation of each of their temperaments.

1—leadership, beginnings, solar, masculine energy. One is very aware of itself, sometimes to the exclusion of other factors in the environment. Generally optimistic and self-starting, but prone to sudden fiery outbursts if frustrated.

2—polarity, lunar, feminine energy, domestic, partner-oriented, emotional, balancing. Two is reflective, introspective, and absorptive/empathetic. Two needs to feel itself part of a larger whole and seeks acknowledgement, like one's own reflection in a mirror.

3—expression, expansion, travel, self-promotion. Three is jovial, fun-loving and creative, given to networking to increase the base of operations and to developing the self for the benefit of the community. It is associated with the planet Jupiter.

4—pragmatic, organized, hard-working, solid, stable, earthy. Four is the number of the material world and of earth in all its beauty. It is the mechanics at work behind Creation, the stage-manager, without whom the show would not go on but who seldom gets recognition from outside itself.

5—curious, active, spontaneous, communicative, restless, variety-seeking, changeable. Five is the centre of the cycle, the pivotal point of the base numbers 1 - 9. Too changeable to pin down, five is always looking for new ways to go forward. It is associated with the planets Uranus and Mercury, and may signify mental brilliance.

6—responsibility, duty, negotiation, balance, harmony, family, aesthetic, domesticity. Six is loving and care-giving, guardian of the Arts and sentinel at the bridge between the strictly personal numbers (1-6) and the transpersonal 7, 8 & 9. It is associated with the planet Venus.

7—aloneness, structure, discipline, review, education, travel, associated with work. Seven is grace, culture, and refinement, tending to work best alone and in its own time. Seven is a measure of time and concerns itself with precision. It is related to the planet Saturn and favors maturity. It concerns itself with religiosity.

8—power, strength, magnitude, influence, philosophy in action, order. This is the number of business empires. Eight does nothing in a small way but is very noticeable, its main theme being power and the correct and responsible development and use of it. Eight is related to the planets Pluto and Mars, signifying energy, destruction and resurrection.

9—completion, endings, release, overview, ideal. Nine is the culmination of all other numerical experiences and the guardian of rebirth. It is elegance, playfulness, imagination, dreams and vision. Nine concerns itself with spirituality and the nature of divinity. It is associated with the planet Neptune and the ethereal realms.

Appendix D
Pronunciation Guide

G aelic is no easy language to get your tongue around if you are accustomed to reading English. Here is a guide to the Celtic names of the four great Sabbats:

SAMHAIN—sow-in (Irish Gaelic), emphasis of the first syllable, meaning "November," but occuring October 31st.

IMBOLG—immol'g, with a drag between the l and the g, like immolug, but with less stress. Emphasis on the second syllable. Also called Candlemass, February 2nd.

BEALTAINE—b'yol-tinna, emphasis on the second syllable, meaning "May." Anglicized to Beltain or Beltane, April 30th.

LUGHNASADH—loo-na-sa, emphasis of the first syllable, meaning "honoring Lugh," (rhymes with Hugh). Simplified Irish Gaelic, Lunasa, means "August." Anglicized to Lammas, August 1st.

Interspaced with these festivals are the solstices and the equinoxes. Together they constitute the Great Wheel of the Year.

The following are pronunciations of the thirteen Celtic tree/month names:

BETH—beh (Birch) B

LUIS—loo-ish (Rowan) L

FEARN—fair-un (Alder) F

SAILLE—sahl'yeh (Willow) S

HUATHE—hoh'uh (Hawthorn) H

DUIR—der, dur (Oak) D

TINNE—chihn'uh (Holly) T

COLL—cull (Hazel) T

MUIN—muhn (Vine) M

GORT—gor'it (Ivy) G

NGETAL—nyettle, ing-tal (Reed) Ng

STRAIF—strauf (Blackthorn) SS (Z)

RUIS—roush, roo-ish (Elder) R

Some other points of interest:

The tree alphabet name, "Ogham," is pronounced owam, or ohm.

Archaic Irish pronounciation of F is as a V, the F is spoken as a W (archaic Gaelic).

If a T preceedes E or I it is pronounced as the Ch (ty) sound.

O = uh.

R, or L adds a slight "1/2 syllable" to a word. (eg. "Gort" = Gor-it)

"Çonoring Lugh," (rhymes with Hugh). Simplified Irish Gaelic, Lunasa, means "August." Anglicized to Lammas, August 1st.

Bibliography

ALDINGTON, RICHARD & DELANO AMES: *New Larousse Encyclopedia of Mythology*, Middlesex, England, The Hamblyn Publishing Group Ltd., 1959, 1982

BREMNESS, LESLEY: *The Complete Book of Herbs*, Montreal, The Reader's Digest Association (Canada) Ltd., 1989

BRIGGS, KATHERINE M. and TONGUE, RUTH L.: *Folktales of England*, The University of Chicago Press, Chicago, 1965

BUDAPEST, Z.: *The Grandmother of Time*, Harper & Row, San Francisco, CA

CAMPBELL, JOSEPH: *Occidental Mythology*,

CAMPBELL, JOSEPH with BILL MQYERS: *The Power of Myth*, New York, Doubleday, 1988

CHETWYND, TOM: *A Dictionary of Sacred Myth*, London, Unwin Paperbacks, 1986

CROSSLEY-HOLLAND, KEVIN: *Northern Lights*, Saber & Saber Limited, London, 1987

DEGH, LINDA: *Folktales of Hungary*, The University of Chicago Press, Chicago, 1965

EISLER, RIANE: *The Chalice and the Blade*, San Francisco, Harper Collins, 1987

ELIADE, MIRCEA,: *Shamanism*, Princeton University Press, NY, 1964

EVANS, ARTHUR: *The God of Ecstasy*, St. Martin's Press, NY, 1988

FARRAR, JANET and STEWART: *The Witches' Bible Compleat*, Magickal Childe, NY, 1984
 • *The Witches' God*, Custer, Washington, Phoenix Publishing, Inc., 1989
 • *The Witches' Goddess*, Custer, Washington, Phoenix Publishing Inc., 1987

FORREST, STEVEN: *The Inner Sky*, New York, Bantam Books, 1984

GEORGE. DEMETRA (with Douglas Bloch): *Asteroid Goddesses*, San Diego, California, ACS Publications, Inc., 1986
 • *Mysteries of the Dark Moon*, San Francisco, Harper Collins, 1992

GIMBUTAS, MARIJA: *The Language of the Goddess*, Harper & Row Publishers, 1989
 • *The Gods and Goddesses of Old Europe*, University of California Press, Berkeley, 1974

GLASS-KOENTOP, PATTALEE: *Year of Moons, Season of Trees*, St. Paul, Minnesota, Llewellyn Publications, 1991

GIMBUTAS, MARIJA: *The Language of the Goddess*, San Francisco, Harper and Row, 1989

GOODRICH, NORMA LORRE: *Priestesses*, New York, Harper Collins, 1990

GRAVES, ROBERT: *Greek Myths, Illustrated Edition*, Penguin Books Ltd., England, 1984
 • *The White Goddess*, New York, Farrar, Straus & Giroux, 1978

GREENE, LIZ: *The Astrology of Fate*, York Beach, Maine, Samuel Weiser, 1984

HANON, GERALDINE HATCH: *Sacred Space;* Ithaca, New York, Firebrand Books, 1990

HARDING, M. ESTHER: *Women's Mysteries*, Harper & Row Publishers, NY, 1971

HILLMAN, JAMES: *Archetypal Psychology*, Dallas, Spring Publications, Inc., 1985

HOWE, GEORGE & G.A. HARRER: *A Handbook:of Classical Mythology*, London, George Allen & Unwin Ltd., 1931

KIRK. G.S.: *The Nature of Greek Myths*, Middlesex, England, Penguin Books Ltd., 1974

KOCH, RUDOLPH: *The Book of Signs*, Dover Publications, Inc., NY, 1955

LARSEN, STEPHEN: *The Shaman's Doorway*, Harper & Row Publishers, NY, 1976

McEVEDY, : *The Penguin Atlas of Ancient History*, Penguin Books, NY, 1967

MALORY, THOMAS: *Le Morte D'Arthur*, Penguin Books, Middlesex, England, 1969

MATHERS, S.L. MACGREGOR; *The Book of the Sacred Magic of Abra-Melin the Mage*, Surrey, England, Aquarian Press, 1976

MATTHEWS, CAITLIN: *The Celtic Book of the Dead*, Aquarian Press, England
 • *Sophia, Goddess of Wisdom*, London, Mandala, 1991
 • *Mabon and the Mysteries of Britain*, Penguin Books, London, 1987
 • *Arthur and the Sovereignty of Britain*, Penguin Books, London, 1989

MATTHEWS, CAITLIN and JOHN: *The Arthurian Tarot,* Aquarian Fress, England, 1990
• *Hallowquest,* Aquarian Press, London, 1990
MEIER, C.A., DAIMON VERLAG: *Healing Dream & Ritual,* Einseideln, Switzerland, AM Klosterplatz, 1989
MONAGHAN, PATRICIA; *The Book of Godesses & Heroines,* St. Paul, Monnesotar Llewellyn Publications 1990
MURRAY, LIZ & COLIN: *The Celtic Tree Oracle,* London, Eddison-Sadd Editions Ltd.,:1988
NATCHEZ, M. and SOLOMON, M.: *The Whole Woman Calendar,* Universe Publishers, New York, NY
NOBLE, VICKI: *Shakti Woman,* San Francisco, Harper Collins, 1991
NORTH, JESSICA: *Runemal: The Ritual of Runeplay,* Victoria, British Columbia: Karma Publisher , 1989
PEPPER, ELIZABETH and JOHN WILCOCK: *The Witches' Almanac,* Cambridge, MA, Pentacle Press, 1991
THE READER'S DIGEST: *Magic and Medicine of Plants,* Monrtreal, Quebec, The Reader' Digest Association Ltd., 1986
ROBERTSON, MARC: *Cosmopsychology I: The Engine of Destiny,* Tempe, Arizona, American Federation of Astrologers, 1976
SCHWARTZ, JACK: *Human Energy Systems,* New York, E.P. Dutton, 1980
SMITH, DEBBI KEMPTON: *Secrets From a Stargazer's Notebook,* New York, Bantam Books, 1982
SQUIRE, CHARLES: *Celtic Myth and Legend,* Newcastle Publishing Co. Inc., Van Nuys, CA, 1975
STAPLETON, MICHAEL; *The Illustrated Dictionary of Greek & Roman Mythology,* New York, Peter Bedrick Books Inc., 1986
STEIN, DIANE: *The Goddess Book of Days,* Llewellyn Publications, St. Paul, Minnesota
STEPANICH, KISMA K.: *The Gaia Tradition,* Llewellyn Publications, St. Paul, Minn., 1991
STEWART, R.J.: *The Merlin Tarot,* Northamptonshire, England Aquarian Press, 1988
STONE. J. HENRY VAN: *A Study in Zodiacal Symbology, Symbols and Signs,* North Hollywood, CA, 1974
STONE, MERLIN: *When God Was a Woman,* Harcourt, Brace, Jovanovich, NY, 1976
TEISH, LUISAH: *Jambalaya,* San Francisco, Harper & Row Publications, 1985
THOMPSON, WILLIAM IRWIN: *The Time Falling Bodies Take to Light,* St. Martin's Press, NY, 1981
THORSTEN, GERALDINE: *God Herself: The Feminine Roots of Astrology,* New York, Discus (Avon) Books, 1981
WALKER, BARBARA G.: *The Woman's Enclycopedia of Myths and Secrets,* San Francisco, Harper & Row, 1983
• *The Woman's Dictionary of Symbols and Sacred Objects,* Harper & Row, San Francisco, CA 1988
WHITMONT, EDWARD C.: *Return of the Goddess,* The Crossroad Publishing Co., NY, 1982
WOLKSTEIN, DIANE and SAMUAL NOAH KRAMER: *Inanna, Queen of Heaven & Earth,* Harper & Row Publishers, NY, 1983
VALIENTE, DOREEN: *An ABC of Witchcraft,* Custer, Washington, Phoenix Publishing Inc., 1973

Biographical Information

Jean Kozocari is co-author of *A Gathering of Ghosts* and *A Witch's Book of Exorcism*. Jean can trace her family involvement with witchcraft back to the sixteenth century. Initiated into the Craft at the age of sixteen, she has remained a practicing Witch all her life. Jean has taught metaphysical subjects at the community college level, and has been a guest speaker on both radio and television internationally.

Yvonne Owens is an author, lecturer, and musician. Born in England of Welsh ancestry, Yvonne embraced the Craft while living in San Francisco, and now lives in Victoira, British Columbia. A member of the Celtic music group, Red Tarn, Yvonne is a collector of traditional songs and stories and folklore. She is author of magical ballads, shamanic stories and fairytales.

Jessica North is a shamanic Priestess of the Old Religion, educator, and psychic mediator. The granddaughter of a practicing occultist, she has devoted her life to the study of Metaphysics. Jessica is the mother of five remarkable children ranging in age from 22 to 4 years old and the is the author of *Runemal,* a study of the runes. Jessica is also a performing musician and songwriter.

Acknowledgements

Thanks to Tara Kozocari for research and contributions, Joy Moon and Christine for reading early drafts of the manuscript, Clint Hutzelock for saving the manuscript from the Abyss, Erin for her art and music, Robin Skelton for his assistance and for the Welcoming of the Bride, and The Thirteenth House Mystery School for bolstering and support.

Thanks also to Vince Klassen for the photography of the masks.